Special guardianship in practice

Special guardianship in practice

Jim Wade, Jo Dixon and
Andrew Richards

Published by British Association
for Adoption & Fostering
(BAAF)
Saffron House
3rd Floor, 6–10 Kirby Street
London EC1N 8TS
www.baaf.org.uk

Charity registration 275689 (England and Wales)
and SC039337 (Scotland)

British Library Cataloguing in Publication Data
A catalogue record for this book is available
from the British Library

ISBN 978 1 905664 99 3

Editorial project management by Shaila Shah, BAAF Publications
Designed by Helen Joubert Designs
Typeset by Avon DataSet Ltd, Bidford on Avon
Printed in Great Britain by TJ International
Trade distribution by Turnaround Publisher Services,
Unit 3, Olympia Trading Estate, Coburg Road,
London N22 6TZ

BAAF is the leading UK-wide membership
organisation for all those concerned with
adoption, fostering and child care issues.

Contents

List of tables

Acknowledgements

The completion of this study would not have been possible without the co-operation and commitment of many people. To all we are extremely grateful.

We would like to thank the former Department for Children, Schools and Families for sponsoring the research and, in particular, Caroline Thomas for her invaluable advice and support. We are also grateful to the members of our research advisory group for their guidance and encouragement throughout the study. Thanks are therefore due to Elaine Dibben, Julia Feast, Jenny Gwilt, Maureen Phillips, Gillian Schofield, Julie Selwyn, Namita Singh and Renee Gioffre, and to Isabella Craig and her policy colleagues at the Department for Children, Schools and Families. Thanks also to BAAF for allowing us to attend a series of thought-provoking meetings on special guardianship for local authority practitioners.

We are extremely grateful for the efficient support provided by the administrative team within the Social Policy Research Unit. A special thank you goes to Dawn Rowley who, with great patience and care, edited and formatted our report in readiness for publication. Also, many thanks go to Sue Clarke for her support with data collection and to Sally Baker, who assisted with data entry.

We are greatly indebted to the many people within the local authorities and national agencies who took part in this study and willingly gave us their advice and assistance. We would particularly like to thank the managers and practitioners who found time in their busy schedules to take part in extended interviews about special guardianship and to complete our survey questionnaires.

Above all, we would like to thank the special guardians and children who took part in the research. Their willingness to help and to find time in their busy lives to complete questionnaires, talk to us about their experiences and deal patiently with our repeated requests for information was truly admirable. Without their willingness to share their views and experiences this book could not have been written.

Notes about the authors

Jim Wade is a Senior Research Fellow in the Social Policy Research Unit, University of York. He has published widely in the area of social work and related services for vulnerable groups of children and young people, including looked after children, care leavers, young runaways and unaccompanied asylum-seeking children. He has been involved in the preparation of best practice guides and official guidance on services for care leavers and young runaways and has acted as consultant to other national and international research initiatives in these areas.

Jo Dixon is a Research Fellow in the Social Policy Research Unit, University of York. Over the past eight years she has completed several research studies on outcomes for children and young people in foster and residential care and young people leaving care. She is interested in the use of innovative and collaborative approaches to working with vulnerable children and young people in and on the edge of care and has published a number of articles and book chapters on care experienced young people.

Andrew Richards is the founder of Second Perspective, an independent organisation providing evidence-based research into practice within social policy areas. During his time as a Research Fellow within the Social Policy Research Unit, University of York, he worked on nationally funded research projects concerned with looked after children and young people at risk of custody. He has published nationally and has presented internationally. His interests now include the well-being of vulnerable young people and the enhancement of under-represented groups in society.

The Adoption Research Initiative

This series brings together the research studies in the Adoption Research Initiative (ARI), a programme of research on adoption funded by the former Department for Children, Schools and Families (DCSF). It is designed to evaluate the impact of the then Labour Government's adoption project, including the Adoption and Children Act 2002 and various related policy initiatives. The research initiative is examining how these objectives are being translated into local policies, procedures and practice.

There are seven studies within the Adoption Research Initiative. They address four broad themes: permanency planning and professional decision-making; linking and matching; adoption support; and the costs of adoption. They also complement other recently-reported and current research on the full range of placements for looked after children, including kinship care, foster care, residential care, private fostering and return home.

More information on the Adoption Research Initiative is available on www.adoptionresearchinitiative.org.uk.

Published by BAAF:

- *Enhancing Adoptive Parenting: A test of effectiveness*, Alan Rushton and Elizabeth Monck, 2009
- *Linking and Matching: A survey of adoption agency practice in England and Wales*, Cherilyn Dance, Danielle Ouwejan, Jennifer Beecham and Elaine Farmer, 2010
- *Pathways to Permanence for Black, Asian and Mixed Ethnicity Children*, Julie Selwyn, David Quinton, Perlita Harris, Dinithi Wijedasa, Shameem Nawaz and Marsha Wood, 2010
- *Helping Birth Families: Services, costs and outcomes*, Elsbeth Neil, Jeanette Cossar, Paula Lorgelly and Julie Young, 2010

Executive summary

Background

A policy priority of the then Labour Government from the late 1990s has been to increase the scale and range of permanent placements for children unable to live with their birth parents. Since the introduction of the Children Act 1989, the main options for permanence with relatives, family friends or strangers have included residence, adoption or long-term fostering. The Adoption and Children Act 2002 introduced a further permanence option for children in England and Wales in the form of special guardianship.

Special guardianship is a relatively powerful legal order. A special guardian is invested with a high degree of day-to-day parental control. Although the order does not legally sever the child's relationship with his or her birth parent(s), their exercise of parental responsibility is heavily circumscribed and they (or any other relative) are not allowed to challenge the order without leave of the court. Children formerly in public care cease to be so and local authorities cease to have direct powers of intervention, other than those arising from their broader safeguarding duties. Local authorities do, however, have a duty to make provision for a range of services to support special guardianship households. While the order cannot be challenged without leave of the court, there are no restrictions on parents or other relatives applying for contact, prohibited-steps or specific-issues orders, unless their right to do so is restricted by the court. In these respects, those obtaining special guardianship have a more limited legal relationship with the child and less protection against further litigation than do those who adopt.

Study design

From a research perspective, very little is known about how special guardianship is working out in practice. This research, commissioned as part of a wider study of permanent placements for children, had three principal aims.

1. To describe how eight local authorities were implementing special guardianship, to account for variations in approach and to identify issues of policy, procedure and resources that have arisen in the first two years.
2. To explore how these provisions were being used through analysis of the characteristics, circumstances and motivations of carers and children.
3. To describe the experiences of those seeking special guardianship, including aspects of their experience, progress and support both before and after the granting of an order.

The research design comprised three key elements.

- A policy study based on document analysis and key informant interviews with 38 managers in eight local authorities and with 10 informants from national child welfare and legal agencies.
- A survey of special guardianship applicants and their social workers in the eight areas, comprising information on 81 carers caring for 120 children.
- Case study interviews with 15 special guardians and, where feasible, their children (3).

An advantage of combining this research with the wider study of adoptive and long-term foster placements is that it provided an opportunity to make some initial comparisons between children entering special guardianship households with children in other forms of long-term permanent placement.

Implementation

There is a high degree of goodwill towards special guardianship amongst child welfare professionals. Most recognise the need for a legal order of this kind and feel that it can provide a sufficient degree of permanence for those who want this. Overwhelmingly, carers in the study also welcomed it. Despite continuing concerns about financial security and the availability of services, most felt it was broadly meeting their expectations and had been the right decision for them and their child(ren).

The degree to which these local authorities had risen to the challenges of implementing special guardianship was highly variable. Some had prepared well in advance, others had been more reluctant to invest time and resources. A key factor that influenced change was the presence (or otherwise) of a strong sense of corporate leadership and of lead officers to "champion" change. Other factors included area demographics, the pressure from other competing priorities, the time needed to scope demand for services and changes required to prevailing staff cultures and practices.

Differences were also evident in the structure and organisation of teams. Each authority had different arrangements for responding to applications. Only in one area did a single team handle all referrals through to the final court hearing. In other areas, arrangements depended on the type of case and often involved a patchwork of teams handling different aspects of the process. A similar diversity existed in the organisation of post-order services. Where a dedicated social work team was involved at all stages (before and after the hearing), pathways for carers seemed clearer, expertise was more readily accumulated, and services tended to be more coherent and comprehensive. As with adoption and kinship care, therefore, there is a case for specialisation where numbers warrant it.

Take-up – who is applying and why?

Most take-up in the first two years had been from relatives (86%), with grandparents in the majority. The children concerned were relatively young, with 52 per cent aged five or under. Most (74%) had been living with their carer before application, often for a lengthy period.

Over two-thirds (70%) had been looked after immediately before application, just under half (48%) in kinship foster care and the remainder in unrelated foster care. Smaller proportions had been living with relatives on residence orders (16%) or without a legal order (14%). Most children had come from troubled family backgrounds marked by maltreatment and parental difficulties (mental health and/or substance misuse problems and, to a lesser degree, domestic violence).

Special guardianship was therefore being used with a broad range of children. Most cases had occurred in the public law arena, either as an exit strategy from care or as an alternative to care and possibly, for the youngest children, adoption. Although carers were strongly motivated by a desire to provide a stable and permanent home, to have greater parental control and legal security, a desire to keep children within the family network or return them to it from care figured with equal prominence.

All things being equal, keeping children within the family network is likely to be beneficial. However, the profile of carers and children raise important questions about the durability of placements as carers and children age, the reduced opportunities for permanence should place-ments break down at a later stage, and the resource implications of providing longer-term services to meet enduring needs.

Take-up from unrelated foster carers had been low (13%) due largely to concerns about financial uncertainty, the potential loss of social work support for them and/or their child, and the potential difficulties of man-aging birth family relationships. In response, some areas were beginning to offer guaranteed financial and support packages for the duration of placement, rather than just for two years as specified in guidance.

While there were encouraging signs of take-up within some minority ethnic communities, there was little evidence that unaccompanied asylum-seeking children had yet been considered.

Pathways to special guardianship

The appropriateness of a family placement will depend on the quality of assessment undertaken and the safeguards that exist to quality assure these decisions. In these respects, the findings were mixed. Carers placed high priority on the provision of reliable advice, information and guidance. This was frequently in short supply, in part due to the newness of the legislation. Where social workers lacked information, heavy reliance was placed on solicitors and the courts.

There was widespread concern among practitioners about the relatively short timescales for completing assessments and court reports (commonly 12 weeks or fewer). Especially where children had not previously lived with these relatives or where children were living with relatives without legal protection, it was perceived to leave insufficient time for depth of coverage, reflection, analysis and for preparation of carers. In these circumstances, some practitioners questioned whether there should be provision for "trial" placements or "pre-assessment" plans for the child, in line with those in adoption.

Most carers in this study, however, had been subject to previous fostering assessments and it is important that practitioners are also mindful that special guardianship assessments can build on these earlier assessments in an efficient and timely way.

Quality assurance mechanisms were variable. In two areas, public law cases were brought to permanence panels for recommendation. In other areas, cases were signed off by senior officers. However, it was not always clear how "private" applications were quality assured, if at all. Given the powerful nature of the order, there is a case for further guidance to clarify and strengthen safeguarding arrangements in special guardianship cases.

The survey findings offered encouragement. Most carers felt that the key assessment areas had been covered in sufficient depth. Indeed, some were frustrated by delays in the process, its overly intrusive nature, and the duplication of information collected by different professionals. Getting the assessment balance right is a major challenge for local authorities when approving family carers. On the one hand, there is a clear need for a robust and comprehensive assessment process to safeguard children. On the other, assessment needs to have a flexible and inclusive format that engages family carers, many of whom will not have freely chosen to resume a caring role.

Once the court decision had been made, the response of carers was overwhelmingly positive, although a minority had experienced some pressure from social workers or the courts to accept special guardianship. Other court orders were quite commonly attached, including contact orders (26% of cases) or supervision orders (11%). The latter had been attached to secure local authority services or arose from court concerns about how carers would initially manage.

Experiences

Most children (65%) had been living with their carers for two years or more at the point of data collection. Most carers (76%) and social workers

(83%) thought that the placements had gone "very well". There were few social work concerns about the safety of children at this stage. Most children were reported to be faring well, especially in relation to their health, attachments and emotional well-being. Overall, well-being was lower for older children and, in some respects, for children with learning disabilities and for those in unrelated foster care settings. Concerns about children's emotional and behavioural difficulties were quite common.

From the carers' perspective, special guardianship was broadly meeting their expectations. They felt it provided sufficient parental control and legal security while enabling children to retain a link with their birth parents. The resumption of care, however, had a considerable material and psychological impact on some carers and their families. Their life plans, especially those of grandparents, had to be adjusted – some had given up employment and most had sacrificed important aspects of their social lives. Although, for some, contact with birth parents was relatively un-problematic, for many others the management of birth family relation-ships was a stressful challenge. Although carers relied heavily (and often preferred to rely) on informal support from family and friends, fault-lines sometimes occurred within families that reduced these sources of help.

Support and services

Given these experiences, many special guardians and children will need some continuing professional support. It was encouraging to find that most carers (80%) had received an assessment of their needs, although depth of coverage was variable, and that these had generally taken place in advance of the court hearing.

Local authority differences in implementation, structure and organisa-tion had made a deep imprint on the services that were provided, to whom they applied and for how long. In areas with higher numbers of applicants, there was evidence of resource strain on post-order support teams, especially in relation to the high level of family contact in these cases.

At the point of data collection, most social workers (61%) were no longer in touch with special guardianship families. In some instances, case closure had occurred very abruptly after the court hearing, despite promises of support that had been made. For others, case closure was not unwelcome. Not all carers wanted or expected continuing support and the value of self-reliance (chosen or enforced) was a consistent theme. The survey pointed to some priority areas for carers. Apart from advice, information and financial assistance, it highlighted the value of support to help guardians manage often complex and conflicted family relationships, therapeutic input linked to maltreatment and the behavioural needs of children, and for support groups, training and social activities. One-third of children (34%) had received some therapeutic input, mainly from CAMHS, and well over half (61%) of carers had received some help with birth family contact. Training needs had been particularly ill-considered during assessment and very little use had been made of respite services (6%).

Specialist teams tended to have a wider range of informal strategies for staying in touch with carers, including informal support groups, newsletters and social events. These provided easier routes back into services when needed. Informality and flexibility are important. Family carers can be reluctant to seek help due to fears of being perceived as not coping and simply providing a signpost to a duty service, as was often the case, is likely to be insufficient.

Arrangements for providing financial assistance varied considerably across the local authorities – and within them with respect to different kinds of applicants. In general, entitlements for former foster carers (unrelated and kinship) tended to be greater. For these carers, allowances were more likely to be protected for at least two years and, in some cases, for the duration of placement. Entitlements, if they existed at all, were much more varied for carers of children not previously looked after or not previously known to children's services. The benchmarking of payments was also not consistent. In some areas they were linked to more generous fostering rates (as advised in guidance and case law)[1], in others to adoption or residence allowances. Inconsistency was therefore the norm.

The survey findings offered some encouragement. Most special

---

[1] See: Department for Education and Skills (2005) *Special Guardianship Guidance: Children Act 1989: The Special Guardianship Regulations 2005*, paras 65–66. The relevant appeal court judgement is: *B v London Borough of Lewisham* [2008] EWHC 738 (Admin).

guardians were in receipt of a regular allowance (90%); one-half (50%) had received assistance with legal fees and smaller proportions had received other forms of financial assistance. There was little evidence of carers receiving large lump sums or of carers pressuring local authorities for additional resources. Once account was taken of means tests and other important fringe allowances paid to foster carers, many were still worse off financially. Some kinship carers experienced financial hardship. In some cases, satisfactory agreements were only reached after the protracted intervention of solicitors or the courts.

Overall, therefore, post-order financial and support services were inconsistent both within and between local authorities and many practitioners identified a need for further guidance to help clarify local authority responsibilities in this area.

Comparing special guardianship children to those in adoption and long-term fostering

Initial comparisons with children in the companion permanent placements study reveal both similarities and differences. Of course, differences in the way these samples were drawn make comparisons at best tentative. One inevitable consequence of this was that special guardianship children were younger and had been living with their carers for a shorter time.

However, the average age at which these children moved to live with their special guardians (2.7 years) was very similar to that for children adopted (2.9 years) but younger than those who entered long-term foster care (4.1 years). Special guardianship children were rather less likely to be disabled than were those in foster care or adopted by carers, although the proportion (18%) was very similar to that for children adopted by strangers (16%). They were also less likely to have moderate to severe emotional and behavioural difficulties than children in all other groups, although this may have been a feature of their younger age. In relation to reasons for placement, the background circumstances of children across all permanent placements showed signs of similarity with respect to maltreatment and parental difficulties.

In overall terms, therefore, children entering all forms of permanent placement appear to have a good amount in common with respect to past family experiences and the legacies these are likely to bring in the present. These often appear to be essentially similar children taking different pathways. Historically, the resources of local authorities have tended to focus more heavily on the relatively small group of children within the looked after system. Fewer resources have been provided to those who are diverted from it or those who exit it through family reunification, adoption or residence. There is some risk that special guardianship may follow this route. While it undoubtedly offers a valuable permanence option for some (perhaps many) children, it is much more likely to work successfully if it is adequately resourced and carers are supported to deliver the care that children need.

1 Background to the study: law, policy and research

Introduction

When a child is unable to live with their birth parent(s) or, after a period of time in the looked after system, there is no realistic prospect of a return home, local authorities attempt to find an alternative permanent solution for the child. Since the introduction of the Children Act 1989, the main options for a permanent placement with relatives, friends or strangers have included residence, adoption or long-term fostering. However, the introduction of the Adoption and Children Act 2002, fully implemented from 30 December 2005, has brought forward a further permanence option in the form of special guardianship.

The *Prime Minister's Review: Adoption* (July 2000) suggested that the existing spectrum of permanence options for children was incomplete and identified a group of children who were in need of permanent placement but where an absolute legal break with their birth families was not considered to be part of an appropriate plan for the child. The Review therefore identified the need for a new legal status that could offer greater security than that available in long-term fostering or through residence, either of which could be subject to legal challenge at any time, but without the absolute legal severance from birth family associated with adoption.[2]

The Labour Government's White Paper, *Adoption: A new approach* (Department of Health, 2000a), published in December 2000, identified some of the groups of children that might benefit from the new provision for special guardianship.[3] These included some (mainly older) children in long-term foster settings, some children who are (or are likely to be) cared for long term with family or friends, unaccompanied asylum-seeking

---

[2] The Review was conducted by the Performance and Innovation Unit and is available at: http://www.cabinetoffice.gov.uk/media/cabinetoffice/strategy/assets/adoption.pdf]

[3] The White Paper is available at: http://www.dh.gov.uk/prod_consum_dh/groups/dh_ digitalassets/@dh/@en/documents/digitalasset/dh_4080512.pdf

children needing a more permanent home but with attachments to families abroad, and some children from minority ethnic communities that may have religious or cultural difficulties with adoption as it is currently set out in law.

The White Paper (in para 5.10) also outlined the contours of this new option, stressing that it would only be used where adoption was not considered appropriate and where the courts deemed it to be in the best interests of the child. It would:

- give the carer clear responsibility for all aspects of caring for the child or young person, and for taking the decisions to do with their up-bringing – as the child will no longer be looked after by the local authority;
- provide a firm foundation on which to build a lifelong permanent relationship between the carer and the child or young person;
- be legally secure;
- preserve the basic legal link between the child and their birth family;
- be accompanied by proper access to a full range of support services including, where appropriate, financial support.

Special guardianship is therefore intended to be a very powerful order. It allows special guardians to make almost all decisions affecting the child's upbringing to the exclusion of others, although the legal responsibilities of birth parents are not entirely extinguished. Where the child had previously been looked after, the involvement of the local authority ceases, save for the provision of support and services, and, unlike residence and fostering, the potential for subsequent legal challenge is curtailed unless leave of the court to do so is obtained.[4]

This chapter situates the present study, provides a brief overview of the research and policy background that has informed the development of special guardianship, and provides an outline of the new legal framework.

---

[4]   Birth parents or others cannot apply to revoke a special guardianship order or apply for a residence order without leave of the court and need to demonstrate a significant change in circumstances. However, parents may continue to apply under s.8 of the Children Act 1989 for contact, prohibited-steps and specific-issues orders without leave, unless the court has imposed restrictions under s.91(14) (see Masson *et al*, 2008a).

About the current study

The former Department for Children, Schools and Families (DCSF) commissioned this study on the implementation of special guardianship as part of a wider research study being undertaken at the University of York on a comparison of progress and outcomes for children in three types of permanent placement – adoption by strangers, adoption by carers and long-term foster care (see Biehal *et al*, 2010).

The design and scope of these two components was inevitably different. The wider study was designed to make rigorous comparisons of the progress of children in these three settings several years after their index admission to care. It was therefore a comparative study of pathways and outcomes. The ambitions for the special guardianship component were much more modest. The provisions were new and had only been available to carers from the beginning of 2006. There had therefore been virtually no previous research on the operation of special guardianship (see only Hall, 2008) in contrast to the extensive literature on fostering and adoption. In consequence, the special guardianship study was exploratory in approach, opening up new territory for investigation, looking at how the new provisions were being used over the first two years of its implementation, charting the experiences of those seeking special guardianship, and seeking greater clarity on the issues facing local authorities, practitioners, carers and children. Although there is a need for a longer-term follow-up of children in special guardianship families to explore pathways and outcomes, this study at this time could not provide it.

Research context

A growing body of research has attempted to weigh the advantages and disadvantages of different approaches to securing permanence for children and to identify barriers to achieving permanence for children entering the looked after system. These studies have also been helpful in identifying some groups of children that may benefit from special guardianship and findings from them have fed into the legislative and policy arenas.

A number of studies have indicated that adoptive placements tend to be less vulnerable to disruption than long-term foster placements and that adopted children generally feel a greater sense of security and belonging than do those who remain in long-term foster care (Triseliotis, 2002; Rushton, 2003). Studies have also consistently pointed to the challenge of providing stability and continuity for looked after children in foster settings (Packman and Hall, 1998; Shaw, 1998; Jackson, 2002). Once age and initial status at placement are taken into account, however, the differences between adoption and long-term fostering with respect to stability have appeared less clear cut (Fratter et al, 1991; Sinclair et al, 2005b). The striking quality of the relationships that children and carers are able to develop in long-term foster settings has also been well documented (Beek and Schofield, 2004).

Nonetheless, it has been an enduring challenge for foster care to provide permanence for children, if this is defined as providing a stable family base and enduring relationships between caregivers and young people into adulthood (Ward and Skuse, 2001; Lowe et al, 2002; Triseliotis, 2002; Schofield et al, 2007). Studies have generally found that, when young people leave care at or before 18 years of age, these relationships have too often been fractured and that continuing support from foster carers has very often been limited (Biehal et al, 1995; Sinclair et al, 2005a; Wade, 2008). It is this perceived gap in permanence between fostering and adoption that special guardianship, at least in part, is intended to fill – even though special guardianship orders cease to have legal effect once a child reaches the age of majority.

Some groups of children have been identified for whom adoption is perhaps not desirable, feasible or appropriate and who may therefore benefit from the protection afforded by an alternative legally secure status.

- It is well established that the likelihood of being adopted recedes with age. Although the potential for placing older children has improved, finding adoptive placements for children over the age of five or six remains problematic (Lowe et al, 2002; Thoburn, 2002; Sinclair et al, 2007).
- Some older children looked after in foster placements express a desire for greater security with their carers. Although adoption by carers

could be expanded if the barriers to doing so were lessened, as we have seen, not all fostered children want to break formally the links they have with their birth families (Sinclair *et al*, 2005a).

- Adoption may be less likely where children have high levels of emotional or behavioural difficulties, where they have a history of severe abuse or where they have disabilities (Lowe *et al*, 2002).

- Where foster carers have been reluctant to pursue adoption or residence for children in their care, disincentives have tended to centre on the emotional or behavioural problems of children, the perceived need for ongoing social work support, the financial implications of this transition and, in relation to residence orders, the difficulties that may arise through sharing parental responsibility with birth parents (Schofield *et al*, 2000).

- Young people from minority ethnic backgrounds appear harder to place and are under-represented amongst those placed for adoption, in large part due to difficulties in identifying appropriate carers and matching children to them (Lowe *et al*, 2002; Thoburn, 2002; Selwyn and Wijedasa, 2009). While many adults from these communities may wish to provide care, some may find that, culturally, adoption is a step too far (Department for Education and Skills, 2005). Such considerations may also apply to unaccompanied asylum-seeking children, many of whom retain strong attachments to their birth families and keep them continually in mind during resettlement (Wade *et al*, 2005).

Since the introduction of the Children Act 1989, greater priority has also been given to placing children within the extended family network. Although it was not the first piece of UK legislation to emphasise the importance of the extended family, it marked the rediscovery of the extended family after a lengthy period of decline (Hunt, 2003). The growth in use of family and friends placements has been slower than some commentators anticipated at the time (Broad, 2001). These placements now account for around 12 per cent of all looked after children, although substantially more (perhaps 10–20 per cent of those categorised as "in need") are supported outside the looked after system (Broad, 2007). There is also evidence of considerable variation between local authorities in the extent to which family and friends placements are used (Sinclair *et al*, 2007; Farmer and Moyers, 2008).

Placement within the kinship network has also been given further impetus through the *Care Matters* agenda (given legislative expression through the Children and Young Persons Act 2008), which has emphasised the potential of the extended family network as a first placement consideration for children who are unable to live with their birth parents (Department for Education and Skills, 2006, 2007). The *Public Law Outline: Guide to case management in public law proceedings* and, linked to this, the recently revised *Children Act 1989, Guidance and Regulations, Volume 1 (Court Orders)*, which are intended to tackle pre-court delays and the case management of public law proceedings, should also renew focus on the potential amongst extended family members at an earlier stage of local authority involvement (Ministry of Justice, 2008; Department for Children, Schools and Families, 2008a). They may help to ensure that families receive the support they need, including identification of durable family solutions, and perhaps reduce the need to pursue care proceedings where this is consistent with the child's welfare.

Recent research evidence on family and friends care is encouraging, although by no means unproblematic (Sinclair, 2005; Farmer and Moyers, 2008; Hunt *et al*, 2008). Outcomes for children placed in these settings appear to be broadly similar to those for children in other foster settings, but are often achieved in more adverse circumstances. Kinship carers are often more economically disadvantaged, less well educated and less well remunerated than other foster carers. They also tend to receive less training, have fewer parenting skills and lower levels of social work support. In this context, outcomes appear quite impressive and familial commitment and loyalty may help to overcome these disadvantages.

The personal cost of caring for grandchildren, nieces and nephews is often high and families may come under strain (Broad, 2007). Not only may grandparent carers, for example, have to lay aside their own plans for their lives and struggle with their feelings for their own adult children, but also the dynamics of family contact (of which there is more than in stranger foster settings) may be stressful and require careful management (Broad, 2007; Farmer and Moyers, 2008).

The introduction of special guardianship has therefore opened up a new legal option for kinship carers who are committed to caring for a child in the long term and, as we shall see, it is this group that has disproportionately used the new provisions to date. However, these findings should also make us mindful of the particular complexities of caring for children within complicated extended family settings and of the implications of this for the types of assessment, financial assistance and support that might be needed to make this caring role successful. This is the kind of package that special guardianship is intended to provide.

Custodianship

Although special guardianship was introduced at the end of 2005, it is not the first time that a middle ground has been sought for children who needed substitute families but for whom legal severance from their birth families was not thought appropriate. Its historical precursor was called custodianship.

In 1972, the Houghton Committee reported on matters concerning adoption and most of its proposals found expression in the Children Act 1975. Amongst these proposals was a recommendation to extend the concept of guardianship for some step-parents, relatives and foster carers. This proposal found its way into the 1975 Act in the form of custodianship, although it was not implemented for a further ten years (Adcock and White, 1985).

Custodianship bore more than a passing resemblance to special guardianship. It was intended for use with older foster children or with children living long term in the care of relatives. Custodians were awarded custody, care and control of a child up to the age of 18 or until the order was revoked (Bullard, 1991). However, there was a residence period prior to application that varied for different parties and according to whether or not parents gave their consent to the order.[5]

The parental responsibility given to custodians enabled them to make

---

[5] For relatives or step-parents, three months' residence with birth parent consent, otherwise 12 months; for foster carers, 12 months' residence with consent, otherwise three years (see Adcock and White, 1985).

all major decisions about the care and upbringing of children, although it was constrained in some respects. The child's name could not be changed without the consent of parents or the court, the child could not be adopted or taken abroad for a lengthy period without similar consent, and no inheritance rights were attached. Parents could also apply to the court to establish or vary contact orders without restriction. In these respects, it offered less legal protection than adoption and local authorities had none of the statutory obligations that would apply to children in care, although provision could be made for financial or other support services (Adcock and White, 1985).

The delay in implementation proved critical. Custodianship had not been promoted strongly by government and it was introduced in isolation from other major legal reforms relating to child welfare. In addition, by the mid-1980s, the circumstances for children in care had changed. In particular, the permanence movement had raised the profile of adoption and there was some evidence of greater success in finding adoptive placements for older children (Bullard, 1991). Custodianship had there-fore ceased to be at the forefront of discussion and, in consequence, it was perhaps not surprising that it was little used. Custodianship was subsequently abolished by the Children Act 1989 and replaced with residence orders to settle the living arrangements of children in family proceedings.

However, research on the use (and non-use) of custodianship high-lights some issues to be borne in mind when considering special guardian-ship (Bullard et al, 1991). This study monitored the use of custodianship from its inception up until the end of 1988. Most of the take-up was by private carers, the majority being relatives, especially grandparents. Most of these families had complicated histories and had been known to social services beforehand. Carers were motivated by a perceived need for an order to provide a firm legal foundation for their caring relation-ship, either to prevent a child being removed from the family or to establish enhanced parental responsibility as a buffer against parental interference.

Foster carers were more reluctant to accept custodianship, although there was some evidence of carers feeling pressured by social workers and of social workers feeling pressured by management to pursue custodian-ship. Bullard and colleagues (1991) conducted a non-use study to identify perceived barriers for foster carers. Carers' concerns centred on lack of information about how custodianship would affect them personally – worries that the proposed financial allowances would be lower than those received as foster carers, about losing the mediating role that children's services play in managing contact with birth families and about the potential loss of long-term social work support, especially if their children developed challenging behaviours in adolescence. The authors concluded that foster carers might be encouraged to take up orders of this kind (including the new residence orders) if social services provided a back-up system of support services, including adequate financial assist-ance, which could be provided when and if required. From a local authority perspective, this would still be considerably cheaper (and less stigmatising for the child) than the costs of maintaining them in the care system.

Although custodianship withered on the vine, we shall see in subsequent sections that the issues raised by it have a continuing resonance for special guardianship.

Legal framework for special guardianship

The Adoption and Children Act 2002 provides the legal framework for special guardianship. Section 115(1) of the Act amended the Children Act 1989 by inserting new sections 14A-G that placed special guardianship amongst the orders available to courts when considering legal arrange-ments for children within family proceedings. It is a private law order, although it can arise in either private or public law proceedings. In addition, government has also enacted The Special Guardianship Regula-tions 2005 and issued statutory guidance to local authorities (Department for Education and Skills, 2005). In combination, these clarify who may apply for an order, the circumstances in which an order can be made, the nature and effect of special guardianship orders, and the support services that should be made available.

Applications may be made by a broad range of people with an interest in the welfare of a child, including an existing guardian, anyone holding a residence order or with consent from those who have one, anyone with whom the child has lived for three out of the past five years,[6] or a local authority foster carer with whom the child has lived for at least one year or who has the consent of the local authority. Subject to receiving a local authority report, the court may also make an order of its own motion in any family proceedings concerning a child's welfare, including care or adoption proceedings.[7]

Applicants must give the responsible local authority at least three months' notice of their intention to apply, unless given leave by the court to make an application in the context of existing family proceedings. If the court is considering making the order of its own motion, then it must direct the local authority to prepare a report.[8] In all cases, irrespective of whether a child has been previously known to children's services, the local authority is required to investigate the background and suitability of applicants, the circumstances and views of the birth parents and children concerned, and provide reports for the court to consider. The form and coverage of this report are prescribed in some detail in Regulation 21. Local authorities have discretion in deciding how to arrange for the completion and monitoring of assessments and court reports, provided they are undertaken by suitably qualified social workers, and there is no requirement for scrutiny by a permanence panel, as would be the case with long-term fostering or adoption.

Once the court receives this report, it must weigh this evidence together with representations from the parties concerned and any other reports available from officials, such as a children's guardian. As with all private law orders under the Children Act 1989, the court must give paramount consideration to the welfare of the child and pay due attention to matters contained in the Children Act welfare checklist (s.1(3)). As

---

[6]   In the case of relatives, the Children and Young Persons Act 2008 has reduced this residential requirement to a continuous period of one year.

[7]   Applicants must be above 18 years of age and birth parents are excluded from applying. Applicants may apply alone or jointly. If a placement order for adoption has already been made, any person will need leave of the court to apply (see Jordan and Lindley, 2006).

[8]   See *Re S* [2007] EWCA Civ 54.

others have noted, while there are clear features that distinguish special guardianship, residence and adoption orders, the legislation itself provides no clear prescription as to how courts should apply the welfare principle when deciding between the merits of these different orders (Jordan and Lindley, 2006). In effect, these will be matters decided through emerging case law and judicial review.

Special guardianship is intended to give guardians control over the day-to-day care and upbringing of children until they reach the age of majority. Although birth parents retain some parental responsibility, this is heavily circumscribed. Consent from birth parents (or leave of the court) is needed to change the child's name, to remove them from the country for more than three months or to proceed to adoption. On making the order, children previously looked after would cease to be so. In most respects, therefore, the order provides special guardians with the scope to exercise their parental responsibility to the exclusion of others with an interest in the child. Unlike residence orders, the holder is not obliged to share parental responsibility with the child's birth parents (Eddon, 2007).

However, there are some further caveats. It is envisaged that children subject to special guardianship will continue to have contact with many (if not all) members of their birth family, so far as this is consistent with their welfare. When making an order, therefore, the court must decide whether other section 8 orders (for contact or residence) should be made, varied or discharged. Furthermore, unlike adoption orders, special guardianship orders can be revoked. Those who may apply as of right include the special guardian, the local authority (where the child had previously been subject to a care order) or any person who previously had a residence order before the order was made (Jordan and Lindley, 2006). Birth parents or other relatives can seek to vary an order with the leave of the court, but only if the court decides there has been a "significant change" in circumstances since the original order was made. However, there is no restriction on parents or other relatives applying for contact, prohibited-steps or specific-issues orders, unless the court has imposed restrictions on further applications.[9] In these respects, therefore, those obtaining a special

---

[9] S. 91(14) Children Act 1989.

guardianship order have less protection against further court proceedings by parents than those who adopt (Masson *et al*, 2008a). Having said this, the likelihood of further litigation is one of the factors the court should take into account when deciding if special guardianship is the right order for a child.[10]

Nonetheless, a special guardianship order is powerful. At first glance, the ability of special guardians to restrict the parental responsibility of birth parents appears similar to that granted to local authorities through a care order. However, there are significant differences. Unlike the local authority, guardians are not subject to formal complaints procedures, cannot be held accountable for their actions under the Human Rights Act 1998 (since they are not a public body) and, unlike with care orders, birth parents require leave of the court to challenge an existing special guardianship order (Eddon, 2007). A special guardian is therefore in a powerful position relative to others with parental responsibility. The court has to be satisfied that the guardian will use this authority in the best interests of the child and, in order to make this judgement, will rely to a large degree on the outcomes of a thorough and careful assessment process undertaken by the local authority. Establishing what seems right for the child is critical, since the long-term legal relationship formed through special guardianship (especially for very young children) seems more akin in practice to that provided through adoption rather than care orders.

Local authorities also have a duty to make provision for continuing support services to meet the needs of those affected by special guardianship. Services that may be made available to the special guardian, child or birth parents include advice and information, financial assistance, mediation, counselling or other therapeutic services for the child, support with contact arrangements, respite and training to help special guardians care for their children. These are similar to the provisions laid out in The Adoption Support Services Regulations 2005, and the guidance encourages local authorities to develop provision in line with post-adoption

---

[10] *Re S* [2007] EWCA Civ 54.

services. The availability of this service framework represents a distinct advantage over residence.

Where children are looked after immediately prior to application, the child, the special guardian or birth parent may request an assessment of their need for financial or other support services. In these cases, the local authority must comply. Other applicants may also request an assessment. In these cases, however, the local authority is not obliged to conduct one. However, if the local authority refuses to provide an assessment it must provide written reasons and these may be challenged. The procedures for assessment are set out in Regulation 12 and the associated guidance encourages local authorities to follow the assessment process laid out in the *Framework for the Assessment of Children in Need and their Families* (Department of Health, 2000b). The outcome of these assessments and the services to be provided should be documented in a service plan, and the plan should be reviewed annually or in light of a change of circumstances.

However, there is no legal entitlement for special guardians to receive specific services identified through the assessment process (Masson *et al*, 2008a). Where no services are to be provided, the local authority must provide written reasons. Once the representations stage is completed, further remedy for guardians can only be sought through judicial review (Jordan and Lindley, 2006).

Concern about financial assistance was one of the main factors that deterred foster carers from seeking custodianship (Bullard *et al*, 1991). Kinship carers (whether through fostering or residence) have often been assisted historically at lower levels than other foster carers. Although the Munby judgment has led to improvement in this respect, it has not fully resolved the problem of disparity in financial arrangements.[11]

The development of suitable financial arrangements to support special guardianship will therefore be a key to its future success. The guidance acknowledges that financial issues should not be an obstacle to what would otherwise be a suitable arrangement for a child. Regulation 6 sets out the circumstances in which financial assistance may be payable – to

---

[11] *R. (ota) L. v Manchester City Council* [2002] (cited in Farmer and Moyers, 2008, p. 221).

enable the special guardian to look after the child, to meet any particular care needs of the child, to assist with legal and transport costs or to assist with accommodation or maintenance costs for the child. Local authorities should ensure that special guardians access all welfare benefits to which they may be entitled and financial support under Regulation 6 is subject to a means test, the framework for which is set out in Regulation 13.

In general, financial allowances should not include any element of remuneration. However, specific financial rules apply to local authority foster carers. If they received (immediately prior to application) an element of remuneration in their fostering allowance, this will be protected for a transitional period of two years after the order is made. This provision is intended to reduce the disincentives that might prevent foster carers taking up special guardianship and to allow a period of adjustment before a lower level of allowance commences. Of course, there is nothing to prevent local authorities from committing this level of allowance for the duration of placement or from having a consistent benchmark against which to judge the financial needs of all applicants. In this regard, the guidance to Regulation 13 encourages local authorities to give consideration to the amount of fostering allowance that would have been payable if the child were fostered when determining the amount of ongoing financial support that might be required, including the core allowance plus any enhancement payable to meet the particular needs of the child. This would then form the maximum potential payment, subject to the carer's means.[12]

In overall terms – and despite concerns about potential shortcomings in support and services – special guardianship has been broadly welcomed as providing a further relatively secure permanence option for children unable to live with their birth parents (see, for example, Jordan and Lindley, 2006). For its success, much will depend on how it is put into practice by local authorities and on how it is interpreted by the courts. In this respect, some significant appeal court judgments have subsequently been made.

---

[12] See paragraph 65, p18. As we will see further below, this benchmark has now been tested in the courts (*B v London Borough of Lewisham* [2008] EWHC 738 Admin).

Developing case law

Two sets of appeal court judgments, in particular, have proved highly significant and provoked much comment. The first judgment on three independent cases (*Re S*, *Re AJ* and *Re M-J*) sought to clarify the underlying principles to be applied when considering special guardianship orders in the context of adoption proceedings.[13] The presiding judge, Wall LJ, in reaching judgment upheld the decisions made by the courts of first instance. In the case of *Re S*, this was for a special guardianship order rather than adoption, in part influenced by the good quality of relationship between carer and birth parent, in the others it was to support the application for adoption, recognising the need for greater legal protection in these cases. There is not space to consider the judgment in detail, but most commentators have reached broadly similar conclusions about its implications (Bedingfield, 2007; Bond, 2007).

First, there are no legal presumptions about when it is appropriate to make a special guardianship order. The court should address the question of the child's welfare throughout his or her life, paying close attention to the welfare checklist, irrespective of whether the placement is with family or strangers. Each case therefore turns on its own facts.

Second, provided that the judge at first instance has made appropriate findings and correctly applied the welfare principle, appeals against the exercise of judicial discretion in this area of law are very likely to fail.

Third, in view of the inability of special guardianship to guarantee permanency and freedom from future litigation (and Wall LJ noted the weakness of the provision in this regard), the quality of relationship between carer and birth parent may play a determinative role in the court's considerations. In this regard, special guardianship may be viewed as being more appropriate where carer and parent are agreed on where the long-term future of the child should be (*Re S*). It is no coincidence that in both *Re AJ* and *Re M-J*, where adoption orders were upheld, the birth parents continued to harbour hopes that the child would be returned to

---

[13] *Re S* [2007] EWCA Civ 54; *Re AJ* [2007] EWCA Civ 55; *Re M-J* [2007] EWCA Civ 56. See Bedingfield (2007) and Bond (2007) for a summary of these cases.

them eventually. In these circumstances, the greater legal protection afforded by adoption may be preferred.

Finally, a court making a special guardianship order ought at least to consider whether a limiting order under section 91(14) of the Children Act 1989 is necessary, given the freedom of relatives to engage in further litigation. This might then increase the legal security afforded to special guardians.

The second judgment adjudicated on the level of allowances properly payable by the London Borough of Lewisham to a grandparent caring for her three-year-old grandchild on a special guardianship order and on the legality of the borough's special guardianship allowance scheme in general.[14] The grandparent had been receiving a kinship allowance prior to application and was claiming income support, since she had to care for her grandchild on a full-time basis. She was seeking a weekly allowance and financial assistance for a loft extension to accommodate the child and another sibling. The borough had calculated her allowance in line with their new special guardianship scheme that allied payments to their adoption allowance, which was set at a lower rate. The borough offered this basic allowance plus a 15 per cent enhancement to reflect the high physical care needs of the child. The loft extension was refused.

Although the grandmother would have been financially better off withdrawing her special guardianship application, the court agreed this was the best option for the child and granted the order on the understanding that she would seek judicial review.

Black J, in judgment, rejected the borough's argument that special guardianship allowances should be tied to those for adoption (rather than the more generous fostering allowances) because regulations do not permit an element of remuneration for special guardians. Black J felt this was a misinterpretation of paragraphs 65 and 66 of the guidance, which imposed an obligation to "have regard" to the fostering allowance (core allowance plus enhancements) that would have been payable if the child was fostered, since this did not include a remuneration element but related

---

[14] *B v London Borough of Lewisham* [2008] EWHC 738 (Admin).

to the core costs of caring for the child. Black J believed it to be much more likely that those giving guidance intended the local authority to hold firmly in mind the fostering allowance when fixing allowances for special guardianship. In consequence, the local authority's scheme was held to be unlawful. By implication, although outside the scope of the hearing, the judge also queried whether the adoption allowance scheme might also need to be reconsidered.

This was an extremely important judgment that will have implications for the way in which local authorities calculate special guardianship allowances. Those that have based them on adoption allowances will be affected since the court has found that the interpretation of legislative guidance is wrong and that these rates should be calculated in line with fostering allowances.

Summary

- The Adoption and Children Act 2002 provides the legal framework for special guardianship. It is intended to offer a new permanence option for children who cannot live with their birth parents.
- Adoptive placements tend to be less vulnerable to disruption and to offer children greater security than long-term fostering, although once age is taken into account the differences in stability are less clear cut.
- Not all children have equal access to adoption, including older children and those who present significant difficulties to carers. Not all fostered children want it. Foster carers have often been reluctant to pursue adoption or residence due to financial uncertainty and the perceived needs of children and for ongoing social work support. Children from minority ethnic backgrounds have also proved harder to place. Special guardianship may therefore offer a new avenue for some of these children, provided it is assessed as the right option in each individual case.
- The placement of children with family and friends has received greater policy attention in recent years. Although only a minority of looked after children are currently placed in these settings, rather more are cared for outside of it. Given the disadvantages experienced by these carers and more limited social work support provided to them,

outcomes for children appear encouraging but are by no means un-problematic. The personal cost of caring is often high and the dynamics of managing frequent family contact can be stressful.

- The introduction of special guardianship has therefore opened up a new legal option for those caring for the children of others, whether in family or foster settings. It is a powerful order, restricting the rights of birth parents and of local authorities to intervene in the day-to-day care of children. It offers the promise of financial assistance and provision of other support services to assist special guardians to provide care. It also conveys considerably more parental control than that available to foster carers or to local authorities through the exercise of care orders.

2   Study design and methods

Special guardianship represents a major legislative initiative to increase the range of permanent placements available to children. To date, there is limited evidence on how these provisions are being implemented and how they fit with other forms of permanence. This study provides an opportunity to explore the implementation of special guardianship as part of the overall strategy of the previous Government to deliver permanence to children. This chapter sets out the main aims of the special guardianship study and how it was conducted. It describes the referral and recruitment process and provides an overview of the research sample.

As we have indicated, the special guardianship research was funded as a companion study to a wider York study on permanent placements for children (see Biehal *et al*, 2010). The wider study focused on children in three types of permanent placement (adoption by strangers, adoption by carers and long-term fostering). The study therefore explored the different pathways that the children followed through, and in some cases out of, the care system and the outcomes associated with these pathways around seven years later. It compared the emotional, behavioural and relationship difficulties of children in each type of placement, their participation and progress in education, and the stability of their placements. It also explored how the children made sense of being fostered or adopted, including their perceptions of belonging and permanence.

The wider study was conducted in seven contrasting local authorities and employed a mixed methodology, including: analysis of local administrative data on the pathways of 374 children; a postal survey of carers and social workers of 196 children; interviews with 37 children and their foster carers; and focus groups and interviews with social work managers, staff and foster carers in each local authority.

The purpose of the special guardianship study was both different and more modest in ambition. However, a distinct advantage of nesting it with the permanent placement study was that it afforded some opportunity to make comparisons between the characteristics of children entering special guardianship and children in other forms of long-term permanent placement. These comparisons, inexact though they inevitably are given differences in the nature and recruitment of these samples, are described in more detail in Chapter 8.

Research aims

The special guardianship research broadly covered the first two years of special guardianship implementation from January 2006, although field-work was not finally completed until mid-2008, thereby enabling the research to have a rather longer reach. The special guardianship component of the study aimed to:

- describe the different approaches taken by participating local authorities to implementing special guardianship and identify issues of policy, procedure and resources that have arisen;
- explore how special guardianship was being used through an analysis of the characteristics, circumstances and motivations of those who had taken it up;
- describe the experiences of those seeking special guardianship, drawing on the views of carers, children and social workers;
- assess perceptions of its place within the continuum of permanent placements for children and its potential impact on other permanence options.

Research design

The study took place in eight local authority areas. This included the same seven local authorities involved in the wider study of permanent placements (Biehal *et al*, 2010). However, in order to maximise returns from the survey of special guardians, an eighth local authority was subsequently recruited. The areas were diverse in nature – including three London boroughs, two shire counties, two unitary city authorities and one metropolitan district. They were also geographically spread, ranging from London and the "home" counties to the north of England. Although it is not possible to say whether the picture of special guardianship derived from these authorities is nationally representative of all special guardianship cases, it is likely to include a good cross section of cases coming before the courts over the period of study.

The special guardianship component of the study began in July 2007 and the design included three core elements:

- a detailed policy study to provide an understanding of the policy background, different approaches to implementation and issues arising with respect to take-up, procedures, services and resources;
- a postal survey of all identified cases in the eight local authorities where a completed or current application for special guardianship had been made to provide detailed information on motivations, process, outcomes and support associated with these applications;
- case studies of 15 special guardians to provide an in-depth focus on their experiences of seeking and obtaining a special guardianship order, the subsequent progress made by them and their children, and their views about the kinds of services that are (or would be) helpful to them.

The policy study involved interviews with social work and legal service managers in each of the eight local authority areas, an analysis of relevant policy documents, and key informant interviews with stakeholders in national child welfare or legal agencies with an interest in special guardianship. The survey collected retrospective information from carers and social workers involved in all identified applications for special guardianship orders. In the seven original local authorities, this covered the period from January 2006 to September 2007. In the eighth local authority area, recruited to the study at a later point, it included all applications from January 2006 to December 2007.[15] The case studies, involving interviews with 15 carers and three children, were drawn from the survey sample.

---

[15] Future reference to the length of the survey period will be 19 months, since this encompasses most cases and local authority areas.

Sampling

Referral and recruitment to the survey began in July 2007. The survey sample was identified and recruited through our links with children's services managers in the eight local authorities. They were asked to supply us with an anonymised list (linked by local authority ID codes) of all known applicants for special guardianship orders during the relevant timeframe. Representatives in each local authority approached these carers with an agreed letter on our behalf. The letter was accompanied by an information leaflet and postal questionnaire and explained the nature of the research and what carers' involvement in the study would entail. It asked carers to indicate their agreement to participating in the study by completing the questionnaire or, if they were unwilling to take part, to return the questionnaire uncompleted. We also asked carers to indicate whether or not they agreed to us sending a questionnaire to their social worker, even if they were unwilling to complete a questionnaire them-selves. Consent to participate in the case study was sought at the end of the carer questionnaire. If that consent was not given, the questionnaire was returned to us anonymously.

Overall, 178 children for whom a special guardianship application had been sought were identified across the eight local authorities. Differences between local authorities were marked, ranging from four to 60 cases referred (see Table 2.1). Factors associated with this uneven pattern of applications are discussed further in Chapter 4. However, it is fair to report that the total numbers referred to the study may not reflect the true number of applications made during this period. Initial conversations with managers revealed that some authorities did not have a centralised system for tracing all applications, so it is possible that some cases, for example "private" applications, where carers were not already known to children's services, were not included amongst the referrals. Evidence from the policy study suggests that these cases have so far been very much in the minority and that the majority of cases at that time had arisen in the context of public law proceedings.

Subsequent discussions with social workers revealed that not all of these referrals would be suitable for us to contact and nine cases were subsequently removed from the study, in the main because they were considering withdrawing or had withdrawn their application. Of the remaining 169 cases referred to the study, 111 were "index" children and 58 were siblings. Index children were defined as either the only child in the household or the eldest of a sibling group for whom a special guardianship order had been sought.

Data collection

Policy study

The key component of the policy study involved telephone interviews with a range of local and national professional stakeholders with an interest in special guardianship. A snowballing methodology was employed to identify interviewees with a substantial knowledge of the field and included interviews with:

- 38 practitioners with responsibility for planning and delivering special guardianship, long-term fostering or adoption services in the eight participating local authorities (usually at team or service manager level); and
- ten key informants from national stakeholder agencies, including representatives from bodies involved in family legal proceedings, advocacy and rights practice, voluntary and statutory sector child welfare agencies and court services.

These interviews, which included a combination of short scoping telephone interviews and more detailed semi-structured interviews, enabled multi-layered local and national perspectives on special guardianship to be gathered. All of the main interviews were digitally recorded and transcribed. The interviews explored a number of core issues:

- the nature and scope of local provision for supporting the implementation of special guardianship services and variations in the approach of local authorities;
- patterns of take-up and the characteristics of those seeking orders;
- factors linked to the policy, resource or service environment that might promote or inhibit take-up and the adequacy of this environment for meeting the needs of special guardianship families;

- the strengths and difficulties of working in partnership (with children, guardians and birth parents) and across agencies (children's services, health services and the courts);
- the adequacy of the current regulatory and guidance framework for delivering effective services;
- the current (and potential) impact of special guardianship on other permanence options for children.

The policy study also included a review of policy documents relating to the development of policies, procedures and services to support special guardianship in the eight local authorities since its inception. This analysis took account of policies to support permanence for children deriving from the Adoption and Children Act 2002 and focused on how the authorities were attempting to meet the Government's objectives for special guardianship, including arrangements to assess applicants, prepare reports for the court, assess needs for financial and other support services, and deliver these services to the benefit of carers and children.

The survey

Survey data from carers were collected via postal questionnaires. As some carers were applying for special guardianship for more than one child, two versions of the carer questionnaire were developed to limit the burden on respondents and minimise duplication of information. A full "index" version covered information on the carer, index child, application process and post-order experience. A shorter "sibling" version collected child specific data only. Sibling versions of the questionnaire were only sent if the carer had returned an index questionnaire. If they did not return the index questionnaire, we had to assume that consent had been withheld and no further contact was made.

Postal questionnaires were also sent to social workers responsible for managing these cases, unless permission had been refused by carers. Again, a full "index" version and shorter "sibling" version of the social worker questionnaire were developed.

To maximise response rates, two reminder letters were posted to carers by our local authority representatives. The first, sent seven days after the initial pack, contained a letter only, the second, sent ten days later, included a letter and a questionnaire. To boost the response rate from social workers, telephone interviews were offered and carried out as an alternative to the postal questionnaire. If these strategies failed, we had to assume that consent had been withheld.

Wherever it was possible, information was gathered once a final decision on the special guardianship application had been reached by the court. However, this was not always possible due to the length of time between application and court decision or because some cases were referred to the study late in the sampling period. Consequently, some cases (n = 24) included in the study were in the application process throughout the study timeframe and complete data were not obtainable.

The information gathered from carers and social workers covered similar ground, thereby allowing us to gather a rounded view and exploit differences that arose in the perspectives of different parties. The data included:

- demographic characteristics of the child and carer (age, sex, ethnic origin);
- health and disability status of the child;
- relationship of child to carer;
- type of placement and reasons for placement;
- child's progress and well-being subsequent to placement;
- child's contact and relationships with birth parents or other relatives;
- placement history of the child (from social workers only);
- child's past involvement with children's services;
- reasons for the special guardianship application and the circumstances in which this occurred;
- social work assessment undertaken to prepare the court report and assess support needs;
- contact and support for child and carers at application stage from social workers and other agencies.

Where the court had heard the application, data included:

- outcome of application (whether a special guardianship order, or any other order, had been granted);

35

- arrangements made for financial assistance or other support services (where considered necessary);
- social work plans to support or mediate birth parent contact (where considered necessary);
- contingency plans for future difficulties.

Case studies

The case studies aimed to provide an in-depth understanding of how, why and in what circumstances applications for special guardianship were being made and of how the process of applying was experienced by carers and children. A sub-sample of cases was chosen from those respondents who indicated their agreement on the postal questionnaire to meet for interview. Interviews were carried out by researchers in the carers' own homes. Semi-structured interviews were undertaken and all interviews were recorded and transcribed.

Interviews with children were designed to explore their understanding of special guardianship and the meaning this had for them, their perceptions about how they were getting on in their lives and their feelings of belonging and permanence. Interviews also aimed to explore children's feelings about the degree to which their wishes had been taken into account when decisions were being made on their behalf and their feelings about the contact and relationships they have with birth parent(s) or other family members with whom they are not resident. These questions mirrored those being asked of adopted and fostered children in the main study. Because of the nature and content of the interviews, a decision was taken to only interview children aged eight years and over. Where a carer agreed to be interviewed but it was not thought appropriate to interview the child, because of either their age or other circumstances, we carried out a carer-only interview.

Interviews with carers explored their views on:

- the background and history of the child (where this was known);
- the circumstances and motivations that gave rise to the application;
- their experience of the application process and the role of different agencies during this period;
- the arrangements to provide financial or other forms of support;

- contact and relationships with the child's birth parent(s);
- the nature of special guardianship, its impact on them and their families and how it compared to other forms of parenting (adoption, fostering or "ordinary" parenting) where they had experience of these;
- the range of issues that might need to be tackled to make special guardianship more effective.

Response rates

Although 178 children had initially been referred to the study, question-naires were finally sent to 111 carers who were caring for 151 children. As noted above, some cases were withdrawn as not relevant (n = 9) and some "sibling" questionnaires had been withheld if carers had not returned an index questionnaire, which explains the discrepancy in child numbers. Out of these, completed questionnaires were returned by 51 carers caring for 79 children, a response rate of 46 per cent (for carers) or 52 per cent (for children).

Unfortunately, it has not been possible for us to analyse the implica-tions of carer refusals for the nature of our final sample, even though it would be helpful to know whether those who refused to participate shared certain characteristics or experiences. The initial information provided by local authorities was only sufficient to enable us to identify a survey sample frame. Since non-response had to be understood as a signal that consent had not been provided, it would have been unethical to go back to social workers in order to seek additional information about this group of carers.

With respect to social workers, a total of 164 questionnaires were sent out (109 for "index" children and 55 for siblings). Of these, 86 were eventually returned or completed by telephone, a response rate of 52 per cent.

For some children, therefore, we had survey data from both carers and social workers (n = 45). For others, we had data from just a social worker (n = 41) or a carer (n = 34). Overall, the final sample included 120 children who were being looked after by 81 carers. Most carers had been seeking a special guardianship order for a single child (74%; n = 60), but 26 per cent (n = 21) were applying for a sibling group.

There was also considerable variation by local authority in both the number of children referred and the number finally included in the study, as shown in Table 2.1.

The case study sample was drawn from those participating in the survey and included only cases where the carer had agreed to an interview and where a final decision had been reached on their application. This allowed us to trace each case to a conclusion and consider the support arrangements that were in place.

Permission to interview the child was sought from carers. Initially, we had intended only to include cases where the child was aged eight or over. However, this criterion was subsequently removed as relatively few cases (12 of those suitable for the case study) involved children in this age range.

In all, 27 carers agreed to an interview. However, only 21 of these had reached a court decision and were therefore suitable for interview. Difficulties in tracing (where some carers had moved away) or in setting up interviews within the data collection timeframe led to the exclusion of a further six cases.

Interviews were therefore undertaken with 15 carers. All but one had made special guardianship applications for a single child, the other being for a sibling group of four children. Although six of these carers had

Table 2.1

Children referred and children included in the study by local authority

Area	Numbers of children referred to study	Numbers of children included in final sample
1	29	17
2	4	4
3	20	15
4	11	5
5	13	10
6	34	18
7	7	7
8	60	44
Total	**178**	**120**

children aged over eight years, three children had severe learning difficulties. In these cases, the carers understandably refused permission for us to interview the children and we were therefore only able to carry out three child interviews.

Data analysis

The special guardianship component of the overall study is exploratory and descriptive-analytic in approach. Unlike the main study, it was not intended to compare and evaluate different pathways and outcomes. Nor would it be feasible to do so, given the limited knowledge available on special guardianship and the relative newness of the legislation. However, we have been able to provide some comparisons between these children and those in the adoption and fostering samples and these strands are drawn out in Chapter 8.

In contrast to the main study, the purpose of this component was to explore the implementation process and identify key issues that arose, to describe the experiences of those seeking special guardianship, and to identify important factors that appeared to shape those experiences. It describes how these children came to be living in special guardianship families and explores how they were getting on together. It cannot demonstrate whether or not these were the "right" placements for these children, since to do so would require a much longer follow-up to determine how things eventually turned out for them. An outcomes study of this kind, however, will be essential in the future to understand more fully the potential and place of special guardianship in the continuum of permanent placements for children.

Information from the policy study was subject to qualitative data analysis. All policy documents, together with the transcripts of key informant interviews, were analysed to identify themes and emerging issues at local and national level as well as differences in approaches to implementing special guardianship across the eight participating authorities. These data were summarised and recorded on a Microsoft Access database, modified for the purpose of multi-level thematic analysis. Chapter 3 provides a focus on the policy, practice and resource environment and considers how variations in this have shaped the implementation of special guardianship.

Information from the survey questionnaires provided both quantitative and qualitative data on the context, process and outcomes of special guardianship applications from the perspective of carers and social workers. Statistical analysis, carried out using the analysis software package SPSS-16, yielded descriptive data on the context in which the placement was made, the nature of the placement, children's subsequent progress in key areas of their lives, and contact and relationships with birth families. It also provided detailed data on the process and outcome of special guardianship applications, including its impact on family life and the support provided by children's services and other agencies. Qualitative information from the survey was used to complement and enhance these statistical data, by use of comments and case illustrations.

Information from the case study interviews was transcribed and analysed using the qualitative analysis programme Atlas-ti. Analysis focused on identifying key themes across cases that could help us to understand how, why and in what circumstances special guardianship applications were being made, how the application process was experienced, how the placement had been experienced subsequently, and whether and how the informal or professional support received had mediated these experiences. These data were also utilised (in combination with statistical data) to construct more detailed illustrative case study profiles.

The detailed findings from the survey and case study interviews are presented in Chapters 4–7.

Ethical considerations

As the special guardianship component was an extension of the existing permanent placements study, it was conducted according to the ethical framework that had already been negotiated in the participating authorities. Permission was sought from each local authority to proceed with this extension and responses were universally enthusiastic. This ethical framework was implemented in line with the Social Policy Research Unit's code of practice, which has been informed by the Social

Research Association's Ethical Guidelines 2003, the Data Protection Act 1998 and guidance on Research Governance provided by government. An advisory group was established for the overall study to advise on, amongst other things, ethical issues that arose during the course of the study.

All participants (carers and children) were sent leaflets explaining the purpose of the research, what their involvement would entail and what would happen to the information they provided. Guarantees were also provided with respect to the handling, storage and subsequent use of data in line with data protection legislation. At the time of interview, this information was reiterated and it was made clear to interviewees that they could withdraw consent at any stage and that, if any questions caused discomfort, they were at perfect liberty not to answer or to take a break from the interview. A guarantee of confidentiality was provided to all participants and it was made clear that no agencies, professionals, carers or children would be identified in any products of the research. In this light, some case study material has been altered to protect identities and any names used in the text are entirely fictitious. The only exception to the confidentiality guarantee would be in circumstances where a child (or another child) was reported to be at significant risk of harm. This was made clear at the outset of interviews and in the advanced information sent to participants. Fortunately, this situation did not arise during the course of the fieldwork.

Summary

- The special guardianship component of the study began in July 2007 and included eight local authorities – the same seven local authorities as the wider study plus an additional area added to increase sample size. The component broadly covers the first two years of implementation of special guardianship.
- The research comprised three key elements: a policy survey that included interviews with key informants at local and national level and analysis of relevant policy and procedure documents; a postal survey of carers who had applied for special guardianship during the study timeframe (for most, January 2006 to September 2007) and a parallel survey of social workers responsible for these cases; and case

studies involving in-depth interviews with carers and, where appropriate, children.

- In total, 178 children subject to special guardianship applications were identified across the eight local authorities – ranging from four cases in one area to 60 in another – indicating regional variation in the use of special guardianship.

- Postal questionnaires sent to carers yielded a 52 per cent response rate for children (46% for carers). The same percentage of social workers (52%) returned a questionnaire.

- The final study sample consisted of 81 carers caring for 120 children. The survey returns came from a combination of both carer and social worker (n = 45), social worker only (n = 41) or carer only (n = 34).

- Case study interviews were conducted with 15 special guardians and three children. The low number of children interviewed was related to their young age or, in three cases, their learning disabilities.

3 Implementing special guardianship: policy, practice and resources

I think [special guardianship] will offer children permanence. For a number of children who have links with their family, it will certainly offer them a sense of permanence that they cannot get [through] long-term fostering. It is also slightly different, I think, than a residence order, in that . . . the mammoth share of parental responsibility is with the guardian, and so it is probably as near as you can get to adoption without severing legal links with the birth family and, for a number of children, I do think that's the right way forward. (Head of adoption service)

This chapter reviews findings from policy interviews conducted with 38 managers and practitioners across the eight local authorities and with ten stakeholders in national agencies with a leading interest in special guardianship. The chapter draws together their (sometimes differing) perceptions about the progress that has been made over the first two years of special guardianship and about their experience of working with it. It also draws on an analysis of relevant policy documents forwarded by these authorities. Most would concur with the view presented above about the potential of special guardianship to meet the needs of certain groups of children requiring permanent placement. There is a considerable degree of good will towards this relatively new provision, albeit with a fair sprinkling of caution about how it might work effectively and with whom. If much of the discussion that follows centres on the challenges and difficulties involved in making special guardianship work, we should not lose sight of the fact that most practitioners are sympathetic to its overall ambitions.

Implementation: variations in the speed of change

It is unlikely to come as a major surprise to find (as we did) that there was considerable variation in the speed with which these local authorities had responded to the challenges presented by special guardianship over the first two years. Some had undertaken preliminary work on the required infrastructure prior to implementation in December 2005 and were effectively "ready to go"; others were more reticent or distracted by a range of competing pressures and priorities. As we have seen, these variations were reflected (at least in part) in the number of children referred to us from different areas, ranging from four to 60. These differences appear quite large over a period of approximately 21 months.

Variations in the use of special guardianship across local authorities (and in the services associated with it) are also likely to continue. Area demographics will play their part. The scale of applications and the service delivery systems required to respond to them will vary according to the size, location and composition of local authorities. However, recent research has also alerted us to the way that local authorities and the teams that work within them vary in their use of different placement resources. For example, Sinclair and colleagues' (2007) study of children's pathways through the care system found significant variation by local authority in the likelihood that children would become looked after and, if they did, whether they would remain so or whether they would return to their families, be placed in kinship settings or go on to adoption. In addition, these differences had little to do with the characteristics of these children and families and much more to do with differences in the policies and procedures of the local authorities themselves. Similar patterns of local authority variation have also been found in recent studies of kinship care (Farmer and Moyers, 2008) and adoption (Biehal *et al*, 2010). So variation appears to be the norm.

The policy interviews highlighted a number of factors that had influenced the implementation of special guardianship in our local authorities. Most important amongst these appeared to be the degree to which local authorities had developed a sense of corporate leadership with senior lead officers who could "champion" special guardianship and initiate change. In areas where this strategic leadership was evident, greater progress had been made at an early stage to develop appropriate policies and procedures, identify required resources, provide training and information, and develop repositories of expertise. Where leadership was lacking, progress tended to be slow and was less likely to become embedded in local practice:

I don't think we've made as much progress as we would have liked. I think the situation would have been helped if we had been able to pull together policies much sooner, in particular, around the financial arrangements . . . I think there may well have been a need to do a little more preparation prior to the onset of special guardianship . . . I wouldn't say there's been a particularly strong corporate leadership on this particular subject. (Team manager, looked after children)

Of course, there tends to be a reciprocal relationship between demand and service development. In areas where interest in special guardianship had been low, the pressure on local authorities to develop an infrastructure to support its development was also consequently low. In contrast, areas that had given special guardianship a higher strategic priority had tended to stimulate demand, by ensuring it was discussed in reviews of looked after children and in planning meetings for children "in need", and by cascading information to interested parties (practitioners, carers and families) and other agencies in the local area.

Factors that had tended to slow implementation were varied. All local authority policy makers were resource wary. The potential demand for special guardianship services was an unknown, especially that which would arise from "private" applications concerning children not previously known to children's services. Time was needed to scope these support needs and to establish the longer-term resource implications to which they gave rise. In some areas, it was felt that early experience had not matched expectations. The families coming forward had tended to have more complicated histories and higher-level support needs than had been anticipated. In consequence, one area that had been initially quite generous in relation to post-order support, reported that this was now becoming unsustainable as demand grew.

In some areas, implementation was also squeezed by the pressure of other priorities and initiatives, by major restructuring that tended to reduce rather than strengthen team capacities or by difficulties of owner- ship where services (like adoption support) were shared across a number of local authorities. In addition, implementation also tended to require changes in prevailing cultures and assumptions about permanence and time for local authorities to clarify their understanding of who special guardianship was really intended for, when it should be used instead of other options (such as foster care, adoption or residence) and the criteria by which its appropriateness should be judged.

For example, there were differing perspectives about whether special guardianship is primarily intended to be for a relatively small group of children settled with foster carers or relatives whose care can be adequately met (in the main) independently of long-term local authority support, or whether it might be used successfully with a broader range of children who, in other circumstances, might have become looked after or gone on to adoption. These are important questions, the answers to which are likely to have a bearing on the nature and level of services provided by local authorities. They also have a bearing on where responsibility for special guardianship might sit within local authorities and on whether investment is made in a specialist service or whether it continues to reside within a patchwork of more generic services for children and families.

Developing an organisational and procedural framework

There is . . . an issue . . . about whether there's a proper service set up or whether it's . . . a service that's [provided] in a slightly ad hoc way by field social workers . . . I think where you've got a specialist team looking at it . . . it's going to be much more effective than when it's . . . delivered in bits. (National voluntary agency)

The special guardianship regulations and guidance are not prescriptive about how local authorities should structure their services, although they are encouraged to 'take into account' other similar services, such as adoption support, when planning their provision (Department for Education and Skills, 2005, p. 9). There was a considerable degree of consensus amongst interviewees from national agencies about the lack of consistency in approach between local authorities. Specialist teams were thought to provide clearer lines of responsibility and to facilitate the development of pools of expertise that other practitioners could draw upon when needed. Services were also perceived to be more coherent and comprehensive. Where services were decentralised within fostering teams, looked after children and/or children in need teams, pathways and services for applicants were considered to be more fragmented. For external professionals and families, effective communication was often more difficult and basic information about procedures, entitlements and services often appeared hard to come by.

This variety in approach existed across our eight local authorities. Each local authority had different arrangements for referral and for pre-order services (assessments and court reports). Only in one area did a single team (the kinship team) handle all cases referred to the authority from inception through to the court hearing. In all others, the teams that were involved depended on the type of case. At its simplest, arrangements involved two teams – for example, a fostering team managing cases involving unrelated foster carers and a kinship team managing all other referrals. At its most complicated, a plethora of area-based teams could be involved – including subcontracted agencies, assessment teams, children's social workers, and fostering and family support teams. In these more complex scenarios, it was often difficult for us to find information about pathways for some groups, especially for "private" applications concerning children not previously known to children's services, and interviewees were sometimes confused about where expertise could be found locally:

We are very disjointed in [this authority]. We have lots of different . . . teams that do lots of different things . . . Nobody has one complete view of the whole. (Service manager, intake team)

Four local authorities had located post-order support services in a specialist team. These services had evolved from rather confused beginnings and different solutions had emerged over time as special guardianship applications and demand for services had grown.[16]

---

[16] The four areas concerned were responsible for a large proportion of the cases referred to us – ranging from 15 to 60 children over the sampling period.

One area (with the highest number of referrals) had developed a dedicated special guardianship team; two others had located services within their post-adoption teams; and the other, reflecting the preponderance of applications from relatives, in a new kinship team. In areas where demand had been lower, service arrangements remained more diffuse. However, in some of these areas; discussions were continuing about strategies to realign post-order services in the future.

The regulations and guidance identify the broad range of adults who may apply for special guardianship. In addition, the court may grant an order of its own motion in the context of any family proceedings (Department for Education and Skills, 2005, p. 6). The nature of special guardianship as a private law order means that local authorities are not always in the driving seat and, in consequence, the pathways by which special guardianship applications first come to the attention of local authorities are potentially varied. In many instances, "private" applications were initially received through legal teams and then passed on to relevant teams (or external agencies) for allocation. Applications concerning looked after children or children in need tended to arise through review and planning systems. In these cases, work was then either undertaken solely by the social worker concerned or referred to a specialist team for allocation, where one existed, and further pre-court work was undertaken on a partnership basis.

Referrals direct from courts often arose in circumstances where local authorities had been seeking care or placement orders prior to adoption. In some scenarios, relatives came forward with an offer to care for the child relatively late in proceedings. In others, the court may have instructed the local authority to undertake an assessment of a relative or to re-assess one the local authority had previously rejected. Several local authorities reported experience of courts overturning their recommendations and directing further assessments:

> We've had a number of occasions where we've turned down family members and the courts have re-instructed an independent social worker . . . and then made us pay for it. (Service manager, placements)

This pattern of variety in pathways and service responses was also reflected in concerns across all local authorities about the adequacy of arrangements to provide quality assurance before cases were taken to court. Special guardianship is intended to provide children with permanent placements, at least until they reach the age of majority. Especially in cases involving young children, therefore, placement decisions have much in common with those made when placing children for adoption. Unlike adoption and fostering, however, government guidance on special guardianship does not prescribe how local authorities should quality assure the preparatory work that is undertaken to ensure that placement recommendations are consistent with the welfare and well-being of children. Some local authorities are trying to respond to this problem by creating or adapting existing permanence panels to provide this oversight:

Some local authorities are now setting up special guardianship panels that are non-statutory. The idea ... it's an equity point ... is to make sure that [children] who are going into special guardianship get the same level of scrutiny as [children] who are going to adoption, although the panel process is less formal. (Solicitor, local authority)

The Act doesn't require [cases] to go before the panel. But obviously, if you're trying to develop a robust system that stands up to scrutiny, then in some senses ... you want ... your decisions to be quality assured and that's one way of doing it. (Adoption manager)

Establishing scrutiny through a panel system in special guardianship cases is challenging. Applicants are required to give local authorities three months' notice of their intention to apply and court officials often express frustration if reports are not prepared in a timely manner that meets the perceived timescales for the child. Most of our local authorities were attempting to undertake assessments and prepare these reports within a timeframe of eight to 12 weeks, although capacity issues in teams meant that deadlines were not always met. Many practitioners felt that these timescales were inconsistent with those needed for a formal panel system and that compromises were necessary in the shape of more flexible arrangements.

Permanence panels were used in just two local authorities and even then only in public law cases concerning children looked after or on the edge of care. In the other areas, final oversight was provided by individual senior managers, although professionals were often drawn together in planning meetings at earlier stages. Two of these areas were also considering whether to develop panels involving multi-agency membership to look at cases across the spectrum of permanent placements.

Different procedures were also evident depending on the type of case at issue. Whereas public law cases were more likely to receive formal panel scrutiny, this was less often the case for "private" applications concerning children not previously known to children's services. In some areas, it was not made clear how these cases were quality assured, a particular concern where assessments had been carried out by external agencies. However, in one area where all public law cases went to panel, the lesser scrutiny given to "private" cases was quite explicit:

> *If it's a purely private situation that the local authority is giving a rubber stamp to, then that doesn't come to panel.* (Panel Chair)

The development of local policies, guidance and training to support special guardianship was also variable across the local authorities. As we have seen, in areas where "take-off" had been slow, less investment had been made in policy development and in providing guidance and training to practitioners, carers and relatives. In these areas, such documents as existed tended to restate the official guidance with an emphasis on what local authorities are required to do, rather than interpret and adapt that guidance in the context of local conditions. Lack of senior management capacity was highlighted in explanation:

> *Just so many things to do and not enough time . . . The capacity of senior managers to formulate policy and procedure, getting our heads around the legislation and . . . of making it an embedded practice . . . You have policies and procedures but until [they] become embedded in practice, it's . . . never really implemented wholesale.* (Service manager, fieldwork services)

In areas where there had been greater momentum, a broader range of activities had been undertaken to embed and promote special guardianship. Policies more clearly situated special guardianship within the local continuum of permanent placements. There was also some evidence of policy documents being viewed as dynamic entities, requiring review and adaptation as services and structures changed in response to demand.

Greater attention had also been given to promotion and training. These areas were more likely to provide a range of leaflets and information packs for social workers, carers, young people and relatives. Training was also being used to promote awareness amongst managers, practitioners and panel members and, in one or two areas, preparation groups (modelled on adoption and fostering services) were made available to special guardianship applicants. There was not much evidence of multi-agency training linking children's services, magistrates, solicitors and children's guardians, although one interviewee felt this would be helpful to iron out tensions that sometimes existed between local authorities and court services.

Take-up of special guardianship

There are two sources of official statistics that help us to understand the use made of special guardianship, neither of which are without difficulties. The Ministry of Justice publication *Judicial and Court Statistics* provides data on private and public law applications affecting children in the family courts system. These statistics estimate that there has been an increase in the number of special guardianship orders made during family proceedings, from 474 in 2006 to 826 in 2007 and 1,125 in 2008.[17] However, the lacunae in these statistics are acknowledged by the Ministry itself and have been highlighted by a recent study profiling care proceedings cases brought under the Children Act 1989 (Masson *et al*, 2008b).

The Ministry of Justice statistics are also not entirely consistent with national data provided by the former Department for Children, Schools

---

[17]   These statistics are available from the Ministry of Justice website: http://www.justice. gov.uk/publications/judicialandcourtstatistics.htm

and Families on looked after children. Statistics for the year ending 31 March 2009 suggest that 1,220 children ceased to be looked after due to the making of a special guardianship order, increasing from 70 in 2006 to 760 in 2007 and 1,130 in 2008.[18] Of course, we also need to be cautious about the accuracy of this dataset, based as it is on local authority returns, and mindful that it is silent on applications concerning children not looked after by local authorities. What we can tell from these data is that there is an upward curve in the use of special guardianship and, when local authority tables are inspected, that there is considerable variation in the use being made of it by local authorities – a finding consistent with research studies on patterns of placement for looked after children (Sinclair *et al*, 2007; Farmer and Moyers, 2008).

The White Paper, *Adoption: A new approach*, set out some of the groups of children that might benefit from special guardianship, including mainly older children in long-term foster care, some children in the long-term care of relatives and some children from minority ethnic backgrounds, and unaccompanied asylum-seeking children, for whom adoption was not considered appropriate. Some commentators anticipated that special guardianship would benefit kinship carers as it promised greater security than that available through residence orders, it would avoid the perceived risk of adoption distorting the balance of family relationships, and promised access to financial support and services previously unavailable (Parkinson, 2003; Ward, 2004).

The evidence from our policy interviews suggests this has been the case. There was an overwhelming consensus from national and local interviews that (to date at least) the majority of special guardianship cases had involved children placed with relatives, with grandparents being in the majority. These children were younger than might have been envisaged and most came from troubled families known to children's services. The majority of cases were arising in the public law arena as an alternative to care or adoption or as part of an exit plan from the looked after system. Some children therefore had not lived with these relatives before the order was granted – and this may well be the case for around

---

[18]   DCSF statistics available at: http://www.dcsf.gov.uk/rsgateway/DB/SFR/.

one-quarter of children moving to special guardianship placements.[19]

Many practitioners were concerned that special guardianship was being used in a different way to that which had been originally envisaged and that it was encompassing a broader range of children. Given the age profile of children and guardians, the long-term nature of the placements being made and the likely support needs of the families concerned, some worried about the risks of later breakdown and the subsequent "permanence" implications for children:

The problem with special guardianship is that it is being used in the way that it was not expected to ... for very small children who might otherwise have been adopted. I think there's a strong chance we're going to find out it's failing those children ... When [placements] break down later, those children [could] be unadoptable ... I think you risk losing the chance for the child to have permanence. (National voluntary agency)

I'd envisaged groups of people where mainly ... everyone was in agreement within the family and they would only need minor bits of support ... when they needed it. But they tend to be families in quite a lot of conflict ... And I thought the children would be older, I thought they'd have more established contact. But we've had some very little ones coming through. (Head of post-adoption service)

The corollary of this process of broadening out is that there was very little evidence of take-up by "private" applicants from families not previously known to children's services – from families that might only need minor support from time to time – and this is consistent with the only existing piece of research that used court files to profile special guardianship cases (Hall, 2008). Where relatives caring for non-looked after children were seeking special guardianship orders, an important attraction appeared to lie in the promise of needs assessments, financial support and access to other services, a potential advantage over the postcode lottery associated

---

[19] This applied to 24 per cent of children in this study, a figure consistent with the 24 per cent found in Hall's (2008) research.

with services linked to residence orders. As one interviewee suggested, 'the mantra is, residence order equals no service. That's really what people think who ring us anyway' (Helpline service).

Other groups intended to benefit have also been under-represented. In one area with a significant number of unaccompanied asylum-seeking children, there was acknowledgement that they had not been a focus of attention. Funding was one issue cited. Although these young people are in the care of the local authority, funding is provided centrally through the Home Office Special Grant. Once they leave the system, support and services would be drawn from local authority budgets. A second issue concerned lack of birth parent consent. Although young people themselves could express a view, consent to special guardianship from birth parents was generally unavailable. However, it would seem fair to say that the potential benefits of a more legally secure relationship with substitute carers had not yet been properly thought through for this group of young people.

In contrast, in an area with a sizeable Muslim community, there was a view that special guardianship might prove welcome in circumstances where formal adoption was not.

> *We have a number of families who wouldn't go down the adoption route, it's not appropriate, but they've actually taken to special guardianship really well.* (Service manager, fieldwork)

Unrelated foster carers, however, have been very slow to respond to special guardianship. The reasons cited in interviews were very similar to those which deterred foster carers from taking up custodianship (Bullard *et al*, 1991). Of central concern is the financial uncertainty it brings for the future, especially once the two-year protected period for foster carers ends. Local authorities may also face a deterrent in relation to carers from independent fostering agencies, where the scale of remuneration can be much higher.

Concerns amongst unrelated foster carers (and some kinship foster carers) were also reported to centre on the potential loss of social work support for the child, both now and in the future. For example, the Children and Young Persons Act 2008 has strengthened support for looked after children in relation to health and education. In relation to the latter, it provides for priority access to school places, to school equipment and to bursaries for students in higher education. Considerations of these kinds were thought to be significant for some foster carers. Furthermore, although the guidance stresses that young people who move straight to special guardianship from care will still be entitled to leaving care advice and assistance as 'qualifying' children under s.24 of the Children Act 1989, what this means in terms of discrete leaving care services beyond the age of 18 remains unclear. It is most unlikely that it will provide the strengthened entitlements afforded through the Children (Leaving Care) Act 2000 (Department of Health, 2001). The interviews revealed a good deal of confusion at present that might easily be transferred to foster carers and act as a disincentive to take-up. Further clarification would therefore be helpful:

> *The leaving care stuff is something that needs to be looked at much more carefully . . . As far as I'm concerned, kids on special guardianship, if they were looked after at some point, are eligible for some sort of leaving care service. But I think it's probably the minimum requirement . . . I think this may be one of the reasons that we're not getting more foster carers.* (Kinship team manager)

Another manager, from an area that had supported 35 looked after young people through university, at a cost of around £7,000 each per year, also reflected that most family and friends carers would struggle to afford this unless assisted by the local authority.

However, unrelated foster carers, in particular, were also reported to be concerned about the loss of predictable structures and routines and the responsibilities involved in managing birth family relationships or emergent difficulties in the child's behaviour. While special guardianship may prove attractive for the enhanced parental responsibility it brings and the freedom from local authority interference it implies, taking "ownership" of all decisions affecting the child and being the sole repository of information for birth parents places foster carers in a very different situation:

As a stranger foster carer, you've constructed a world in which your relationship, your customer if you like, is the local authority and your relationship is with them . . . So if the parents aren't happy with contact, it's the local authority that deals with it . . . Going back to the Prime Minister's Review back in 2000, people were saying . . . this will empower carers to make decisions for themselves, and it does, but you then have to own the decisions you've made for yourself and not everyone wants to be in that position. Clearly . . . you're in a powerful position, legally you can restrict the parent's exercise of parental responsibility, but it's your problem and you have to own that. I think for stranger foster carers . . . that's quite a big hurdle to overcome, because it's not what they signed up for. (Child care solicitor)

Growing awareness of the complexities inherent in these barriers has led some local authorities to strengthen the financial and support packages they provide to unrelated foster carers in an effort to make special guardianship a more attractive option.

Pre-order services

Before the court is able to grant a special guardianship order, it must receive a timely local authority report evaluating the background and suitability of applicants and the views and circumstances of children and their birth parents.[20] The coverage of this report is prescribed in Regulation 21 (Department for Education and Skills, 2005). Applicants may also request the local authority to undertake an assessment of their need for financial or other forms of support. Where the child had been looked after immediately prior to application, the local authority is then obliged to conduct one. Where they were not, there is no obligation to do so, although reasons for refusal must be provided in writing and time given for representations. The scope of this assessment is provided in Regulation 12. While there is no entitlement for special guardians to receive specific services identified through the assessment process

---

[20] *Re S* [2007] EWCA Civ 54.

(Masson *et al*, 2008a), local authorities do retain a duty of care and failure to meet this can be subject to challenge through judicial review. Where local authorities intend to provide services, they must prepare a written support plan that is then subject to annual review.

These are complex tasks that need to be undertaken within a relatively short timeframe. As we have seen, service organisation across the local authorities was highly variable. In some areas, issues related to resources and team capacities meant that pre-court services were contracted out, thereby raising concerns about the variable quality of assessments undertaken and the adequacy of quality assurance mechanisms before proceeding to court.

The majority of kinship placements are initiated by carers and children themselves. Local authority assessments of kinship carers therefore tend to be reactive, frequently undertaken once the child is already *in situ*, and the quality of assessments that are then undertaken tend to lack consistency (Broad, 2007; Farmer and Moyers, 2008). In these circumstances, there was concern that some children could be at risk during the assessment period if they had not been placed by the local authority under fostering regulations and no court order was in place at that time.

Where children were not yet living with carers or where care of the child was temporary, pending a final court decision, the assessment process presented significant challenges. Where relatives were caught up in the maelstrom of care proceedings, a comprehensive assessment was often difficult to achieve within the timescales available and considerable time had to be spent in the post-order period revisiting deeper aspects of the assessment process that would have applied to potential adoptive parents:

The first six months of support is crucial . . . [in] making up for what couldn't be done in the assessment . . . What the support workers are often doing is going back over the assessment issues . . . things about attachment, the impact of the child's past history and . . . how that affects the way they should parent the children . . . The more sophisticated issues that are there in adoption. (Team manager, kinship team)

Since the local authority ceases to have a formal role once a special guardianship order is granted, this work can generally only be done with the consent of guardians as part of a post-order support service.

There was major concern that, whilst the short timescales for assessment could bring a sharp focus to the work, it frequently failed to allow sufficient time for in-depth coverage, for reflection and analysis or to ensure that guardians were properly prepared for the task they were taking on:

These children are no different to other children (in care) . . . *They have complex needs and we need to think very carefully about what it means for people to say they will offer a family for a child until at least 18. The thing we know in adoption is that they need information and advice; they need preparation and training; and home study assessments when they are conducted well. That gives people an opportunity to think through their own development and circumstances . . . whether this is the right thing for them and to understand the nature of the commitment they are taking on.* (National voluntary agency)

Leaving consideration of these questions until after the order is granted (if in some cases it is done at all) builds considerable risk into the system and potentially leaves children and families prone to later breakdown, if the implications of this commitment have not been properly digested or experience fails to match expectations. Given the power invested in special guardians through these orders and the limited scope local authorities have to intervene subsequently, unless the threshold of significant harm is met, these were considered to be matters of considerable concern.

The timescales required by the court process also tended to compromise mechanisms for quality assurance through the panel system. While this was used in some areas, in others more flexible arrangements were required to ensure cases proceeded to court in a timely manner:

So ultimately we'd like to go to panel but we're trying to work at the best timeframe that gets an appropriate assessment into court in a timely fashion, whilst trying to introduce some kind of monitoring and . . . approval process within our own internal system. (Service manager, fieldwork)

From a practitioner perspective, it was perceived that special guardianship was primarily intended for children who had been settled with their carers for some time. The higher-than-expected number of children leaving unrelated foster care through special guardianship to live with relatives with whom there had not been a previous period of residence therefore prompted concern. Given the finality of the order, some questioned whether there should be a requirement for a pre-order period of trial placement, as would be the case with adoption:

Unlike a residence order, where there can be an interim order, or adoption, where applicants are not able to submit their application to adopt until the child's been placed for ten weeks, once the court makes a special guardianship order, even for children that haven't been placed with them before, it's game, set and match. They have the higher level of parental responsibility, the local authority's parental responsibility is extinguished, there is only a support role for the local authority and no control. So for untested situations . . . I think it's too much of a leap of faith. (Adoption panel member)

In "untested situations" like these, there was also concern about how adequately the support needs of child and carer could be assessed. The timing of needs assessments is important. If carers are to be adequately prepared for the task ahead and to make an informed decision about the appropriateness of special guardianship for their circumstances, it is difficult to see how this can be achieved unless they receive clear information about the nature and duration of financial and other support services that will be provided.

In most of our participating local authorities, the needs assessment and support plan were prepared as part of the pre-court assessment process. The clarity this provided to carers was likely to be helpful, even if the news was not good. However, assessment in advance seemed more likely to occur in cases concerning looked after children or children "in need" than was the case with "private" applications concerning children not previously known to children's services. In some areas, access to support and services for "private" applicants was unlikely other than in "exceptional circumstances" while, in others, assessments were only undertaken once the order had been granted. This put some "private" kinship carers at considerable disadvantage.

Post-order services

Although special guardians have no legal entitlement to receive specific services identified through assessment, the guidance and regulations place a duty on local authorities to make provision for post-order services similar to the provisions laid out in the Adoption Support Regulations 2005. As we have seen, local authority variations in implementation, structure and organisation tended to leave a deep imprint on the nature of the services provided, the types of cases to which they applied and for how long. Areas that had established greater early momentum and, in response to rising demand, invested in more specialised services were more likely to have developed a coherent range of services. Arrangements in areas that had experienced delayed development tended to be more *ad hoc*. Overall, therefore, service patterns were inconsistent.

Looking across the local authorities as a whole, the potential range of services that were available to guardians and children was quite large, including financial assistance, allocated support workers, support groups, preparation and training workshops, newsletters and social events, respite, access to CAMHS workers,[21] facilitation and supervision of birth family contact, and assistance with welfare rights, health and education services. However, in areas where services were more residual or the number of applicants had hitherto been small, services were more often restricted to signposting clients to mainstream service providers or to accessing services on a child "in need" basis:

We have a very basic support package, basically explaining that support is available through other agencies in terms of health care

---

[21] Child and Adolescent Mental Health Services (CAMHS).

and education etc... They're clear about the fact that they can contact ourselves if they need to look at additional support on a child "in need" basis at some future point. (Service manager, looked after children)

Despite dissatisfaction with the scope and reliability of services, there is evidence that support is generally welcomed by kinship carers and their children (Broad *et al*, 2001). This is consistent with the views of practitioners in this study. Some had been surprised by the high level of service demands made by guardians linked to the needs of children and the high levels of contact between children and birth family members that required supervision and mediation. Some were also wary about the resource implications for teams where courts imposed monthly or even fortnightly contact orders in circumstances where family relationships were not consensual and where these arrangements might last for many years. This was often contrasted with the much lower level of demands made by adoptive parents:

It is totally weird. You'll have the odd one that doesn't want to work with us, and that's fine, but most of them do and are working with us because ... [their family relationships] ... are really complicated. We're asking them to take the higher ground ... and promote contact, when they've seen everything that's gone on up to this point, whereas adopters only read about it in a Form E. (Team manager, post-order support team)

Most of the support is around contact, but the level of contact is much greater than it would be for adoption orders ... [In adoption] your main priority is for the children to make a new family with their adopters and just keep in touch with their birth parents. With special guardianship you're wanting to maintain it ... So it's much more contact. (Head of adoption support)

In areas where special guardianship support had been absorbed into the work of pre-existing post-adoption support teams and where demand for services was growing, there was evidence of considerable resource strain.

In some instances, this was altering the balance of work and the resources available to adopters. In one area, consideration was being given to a realignment of these services to reflect the increase in special guardianship work.

Perceptions about the appropriateness of the support needs presented by these families were also rooted in different views about the purpose of special guardianship. In areas that provided fewer services, it was more likely for practitioners to express the view that it was primarily intended for a relatively small group of settled older children whose care could, for the most part, be adequately met within the special guardianship family. In this view, therefore, while services may be required for a short time to help families settle, the concept of providing longer-term support (other than some financial assistance) seemed anomalous:

> *Social workers are looking at whether or not . . . a kinship carer can be a special guardian for the child. They are assuming . . . that if they're good enough . . . they won't need support services . . . otherwise they probably wouldn't be recommending [it]. So generally . . . in the assessments I've seen . . . there is hardly any mention of services at all.* (Service manager, placements)

> *Generally if a lot of support is expected to be needed, the teams are not wanting to consider special guardianship. They think it should be long-term foster care or possibly adoption.* (Independent reviewing officer)

However, where some services were residual, there was recognition that this might store up problems for the future if families returned for help at a later date but the required infrastructure to provide those services had not been developed.

In contrast, another strand of thinking acknowledged that special guardianship was being used quite broadly and that, by providing a sound framework for the provision of services to families, the benefits for children of leaving the care system or remaining within the family network, provided it was safe for them to do so, might outweigh some of the difficulties presented. Since these difficulties may arise later in the life of the child, service arrangements needed to be long term:

> *Carers [can] become very isolated . . . once children are not looked after any more and they're not Children's Services' responsibility . . . There's often needs that come up later in life . . . and if they're not able to get back in . . . communication or if there's no support on offer . . . I can see that being an issue.* (Team manager, kinship team)

Most teams that provided a dedicated post-order support service offered more intensive support in the early post-order period, in part to complete assessments and to respond to initial needs. Services would then be provided in a lower key, with carers able to dip in and out, unless long-term services were required to meet specific needs of the child or to supervise contact arrangements.

Financial support and uncertainty for the future have been important factors in deterring unrelated foster carers from taking up custodianship and residence orders. Kinship carers have also historically received less remuneration for the care they provide than stranger foster carers (Broad, 2007). Provision for financial support is therefore likely to have a strong influence on the success or otherwise of special guardianship. The promise of assistance is one of the features most attractive to family and friends carers, given their experience of the limited provision available through residence orders (Broad, 2007; Farmer and Moyers, 2008).

The special guardianship guidance and regulations recognise that financial issues should not present an obstacle to an otherwise suitable arrangement for a child. The powers available to local authorities are quite extensive, including payment of regular allowances, one-off settling-in grants and assistance with accommodation, legal or transport costs or to meet the specific care needs of the child. Although financial allowances are generally subject to means testing and annual financial review, and should not allow for an element of remuneration, payments to foster carers are protected for a transitional period of two years after an order is made. The guidance also encourages local authorities to benchmark allowances against the fostering allowance that would have been payable if the child had been fostered.

There was evidence across our local authorities of all these forms of assistance being provided. However, provision was not consistent across all areas or in all types of special guardianship cases. In general terms, local authority-approved foster carers (unrelated and kinship) had greater entitlement. In all areas, payments were protected for two years. In some areas, these payments were not means tested, in others, they were. In some areas, there was provision for enhanced payments (including remuneration) to continue for longer than two years, in others, not. There was also no consistency in how these allowances were benchmarked. Some areas linked payments to the fostering allowance, others linked them to the often lower levels of allowance paid to adopters or those holding residence orders. In these circumstances, the continuing disincentives for foster carers were sometimes acknowledged.

Access to other forms of grant or one-off payment was also more likely in cases concerning looked after children or children in care proceedings. In a few cases, quite large payments had apparently been made to help carers adapt their homes, to assist with legal or contact costs, to meet the specific special needs of children or to obtain a vehicle to accommodate a sibling group. Settlement of these large sums was, in some instances, perceived to be linked to precedents set by the courts:

Once certain things get into the court arena . . . and precedents get set . . . it's [sometimes] cheaper to pay for the car than it would be [to pay for] further litigation or for it to be adjourned [or go to] judicial review. (Adoption manager)

All forms of financial assistance were much more highly variable where children had not been looked after or where families had not been previously known to children's services. While, in some areas, provision in these cases was identical to that for foster carers and benchmarking was consistent across the board, in most it was not. Payments were sometimes made at a lower rate or only in "exceptional circumstances" that were not clearly defined. In a few areas, there was no evidence of any provision at all. Overall, local authorities tended to be much more resource wary about this group of clients and concerned about setting precedents that might have long-term resource implications:

I don't know what other [local authorities] are doing, but we're not paying fixed allowances to children that we weren't involved with before. (Service manager, fieldwork services)

If you start making a payment . . . you might be setting a precedent there. We have paid in private hearings [but] what our procedures clearly say is that it's really for looked after children and/or children who would have been looked after. (Service manager, permanent placements)

It is understandable, in a climate of resource scarcity, that local authorities would seek to draw a boundary around those who count as *their* children – to focus on those to whom they have a continuing obligation to provide support and services. Equally, it is understandable that local authorities would be wary of being pressured into high-cost long-term agreements with families when the scale of future demand is unknown. However, this perspective also exists in some tension with another that was frequently expressed in interviews: that of trying to promote a level playing field across the different permanence options so that placement-making would be based more on the specific needs of the child and not primarily on resource considerations. When carers face high levels of uncertainty about the long-term security of their finances, this can act as a powerful motivating factor for choosing one option over another and, as we have seen, has acted as a major disincentive for foster carers taking up special guardianship. Equally, the promise of financial assistance may attract family and friends carers to special guardianship, given the financial uncertainty associated with residence orders.

In response to this problem, some local authorities are now protecting the financial and support packages offered to unrelated (and some kinship) foster carers for the life of the placement – or until the child reaches the age of majority. It remains to be seen whether strategies such as this will serve to increase the potential of special guardianship for older children in foster care. As yet, however, there is not much evidence of this approach being applied to other children in "private" kinship settings, whose needs may, in practice, be very similar.

Local authorities should also be reviewing their policies on allowances in light of developing case law. Recent judgments have ruled in favour of benchmarking special guardianship allowances at the more favourable fostering rate, rather than at that set for adoption allowances[22] and questioned the legality of paying kinship foster carers at a lower rate than unrelated foster carers when the needs of these children are broadly the same.[23] Whether and in what way these judgments will affect the organisation and delivery of special guardianship services and whether they will help to promote greater consistency and continuity of services are really matters for the future.

National guidance and regulations

The present framework of regulations and guidance may also present some obstacles to the provision of more consistent services. While some interviewees suggested that 'less is often more', reflecting concerns about the micro-management of local authorities, many others felt that the existing guidance was 'too thin'. In the opinion of many practitioners this had created confusion and provided too much room for manoeuvre. Particular concern was expressed about the lack of specified minimum service standards clarifying what financial and other services local authorities ought to provide, whether they should apply to all cases and for how long. This would help local authorities understand what services are required for different groups of children and where service boundaries ought to be drawn:

> *I thought they were a bit thin . . . I think it needs to be more explicit about what [and] when local authorities are obliged to resource and what [and] when we are not. I think it's left a little bit vague.* (Service manager, post-order support)

The broadening out of special guardianship and the profile (especially age profile) of children and families embraced by it, has called for more

---

[22]   *B v London Borough of Lewisham* [2008] EWHC 738 (Admin).

[23]   *R. (ota) L. v Manchester City Council* [2002]; (cited in Farmer and Moyers, 2008, pp. 110–11).

explicit recognition of the longer-term nature of service provision that will be necessary. In light of how special guardianship is being used, some also questioned whether sufficient safeguards were built into the existing procedural framework:

> *I don't think that we have enough practice guidance [or] of a protocol – [given] the nature of it as a private law order and the complexities of managing family and friends care – to guarantee that sufficient safeguards are in place.* (National voluntary agency)

More specifically, further advice was thought necessary to clarify how local authorities can conduct appropriate assessments that take account of complex family scenarios within existing timescales and, second, whether and how quality assurance through permanence panels could be developed further to bring special guardianship procedures more into line with those used in adoption and fostering.

Finally, there was also a worry that, once a special guardianship application was received, the needs of the child and carer could become quite quickly conflated. The thinking of practitioners may proceed along "tramlines" towards special guardianship to the exclusion of other permanence options that may be equally or more appropriate. In adoption cases, there is a need for a pre-assessment plan for the child to establish, in the context of all that is known, that this is the right option for them. No such planning requirement exists in special guardianship to ensure that the best interests of the child are protected. Whether or not such a requirement proves necessary – and it would be difficult to implement in cases where children have been living with carers for some time – it is important that assessments do manage to maintain this separation between the distinctive needs and views of children and carers, perhaps especially when assessments are encompassing sibling groups.

Summary

This chapter reviewed findings from local and national policy interviews on the implementation of special guardianship and highlighted the policy, practice and resources issues that have arisen over the first two years.

Implementation

Variations across the eight local authorities in speed of implementation related to several factors:

- differences in area demographics (size, location, composition);
- the extent of preparatory work that had been undertaken;
- the presence of co-ordinated corporate leadership to "champion" change;
- the time taken to scope needs and their resource implications;
- the pressure of other priorities and initiatives;
- the impact of prevailing staff cultures and assumptions about permanence and of different interpretations about who special guardianship was really intended for. Answers to these questions were likely to affect the nature and scope of services locally.

This variability was reflected in the number of cases referred to us from different areas, ranging from four to 60, in policy and procedure development, and in opportunities for training and guidance.

An organisational and procedural framework

The interviews highlighted the variety in approaches that had been taken.

- In areas where specialist teams had been developed (special guardianship, adoption or kinship teams), pathways for carers appeared clearer and services tended to be more coherent and comprehensive.
- In areas where a potentially wide range of generic teams were involved in special guardianship cases, pathways and services appeared more fragmented and the development of pools of expertise less common.
- Across all local authorities, there was concern about the adequacy of quality assurance mechanisms before cases were taken to court. Two areas had adapted existing permanence panels to provide this oversight in public law cases, despite the tight timescales (8–12 weeks) for assessment and preparation of court reports. In other areas, oversight was provided by a senior manager. It was not always clear how "private" cases were quality assured.

Take-up

- Although national statistics on take-up are not reliable, they do show an upward curve in applications for special guardianship and that rates vary considerably by local authority.
- There was a predominant view that most take-up had been from relatives, with grandparents in the majority. Children were younger than might have been anticipated, most came from troubled families and the majority of cases originated in the public law arena. The long-term nature of these placements and the level of support required had serious resource implications for local authorities.
- There was little evidence of take-up by "private" applicants concerning children not previously known to children's services, and take-up from unrelated foster carers had been low, reflecting concerns about their financial circumstances, loss of social work support and concerns about managing birth family relationships. While there were signs that special guardianship might be welcomed in some minority ethnic communities, there was little evidence of its use with unaccompanied asylum-seeking children.

Pre-order services

- Although tight timescales for undertaking assessments and preparing reports for the court could bring a sharp focus to the work, there were major concerns that they left insufficient time for in-depth coverage, reflection and analysis. In this respect, special guardianship assessments tended to be contrasted unfavourably with those required for adoption or fostering.
- The timescales could build risks into the system, especially where children were leaving unrelated foster care to live with relatives once the order was granted or where they were living with relatives without legal protection. It also meant that social workers were frequently playing catch-up after the event, revisiting deeper aspects of assessment that had not been covered at the time. The powerful nature of the order also meant that the rights of local authorities to intervene at a later point were quite limited.
- In our local authorities, most assessments of need for services were

undertaken in advance of the court hearing as part of the assessment process. This provided greater clarity for carers. However, this was less likely where children had previously not been looked after or designated as being "in need".

Post-order services

- Although local authorities are required to make provision for post-order services, variations in implementation of special guardianship, in structure and organisation left a deep imprint on the nature of services provided and to whom they applied. Specialist teams tended to provide more comprehensive services.

- The potential for financial assistance and other social work services had helped to make special guardianship attractive to family and friends carers. The level of demand, however, was creating resource strains for post-order support teams. Services were also rooted in different practitioner attitudes towards special guardianship. In areas with fewer services, practitioners were more likely to view it as a provision for a restricted group of children whose carers should be able to provide for them independently. In other areas, usually where specialist services were present, there was a perception that it could work for a broader range of families if a suitable service infrastructure was provided.

- Arrangements for financial assistance were variable across the local authorities. In general, entitlements were greater for former foster carers (unrelated or kinship), including protection for at least two years or, in some cases, for longer. Entitlements were much more varied where children had not been looked after or were not previously known to children's services.

4 Carers and their children: pathways towards special guardianship

This chapter traces the pathway towards special guardianship for carers and children who had made an application in the eight local authorities. It begins by profiling the children and their carers and describes the circumstances and difficulties that led to the child moving away from the care of their parents. It traces the journey to their current placements, so far as this is known, by exploring their care histories and past involvement with children's services. The chapter therefore reflects on the ways in which special guardianship is being used in these local authorities, with respect to take-up and target groups, and considers whether the provision is being used as intended in the regulations and guidance. The chapter ends by considering some of the difficulties leading up to the child's arrival in the special guardianship household.

Profile of the children

Special guardianship was intended to address the needs of certain groups of children for whom adoption was not thought feasible or appropriate due to age, cultural reasons or circumstances. The profile of children and carers provided below points to how special guardianship is being used in practice and these findings are broadly consistent with the perceptions of practitioners that were presented in Chapter 3.

As detailed in Chapter 2, our survey of carers and social workers across the eight local authorities provided information on 81 carers who had applied for special guardianship orders for a total of 120 children during the study timeframe.[24] At the point of data collection, a special guardianship order had been granted for 63 per cent of all the children in the study.

---

[24] In this chapter we will use the term "carers" to refer to all special guardianship applicants, as some cases (n = 24) had not yet reached a court decision within the study timeframe.

One-half (n = 60) of the children in our survey group were the sole subjects of an application by a carer. An equal number were part of a sibling group. In all, applications had been made for 21 sibling groups in the study. General information on characteristics and background was collected for all of the children, but some additional data were collected for "index" children only (n = 81, 68%).[25]

Gender and ethnic origin

The sample of children included slightly more girls (53%) than boys. Just over one-half of the children were described as White (55%) and around one-fifth were Black or Black British (21%). As shown in Table 4.1, one-quarter of the children were from other minority ethnic backgrounds, including children of mixed ethnicity, Chinese and Asian backgrounds. Those described as "other ethnic group" included a sibling group of Traveller children.

National statistics indicate that minority ethnic children make up around eight per cent of the population generally and about 23 per cent of the looked after population in England. Minority ethnic children were, therefore, over-represented in the study, accounting for nearly half of the

Table 4.1
Child's ethnic origin

Ethnic group	Number	Percentage
White	66	55
Black or Black British	25	21
Asian	5	4
Mixed White and Black Caribbean/African	16	13
Other mixed	5	4
Chinese	1	1
Other ethnic group	2	2
Total	**120**	**100**

---

[25] Index child refers to the only child or the eldest of a sibling group for which special guardianship had been sought.

sample (45%). This might well reflect the population of the local authority areas concerned. There was certainly an area effect, with three local authorities accounting for 93 per cent of the minority ethnic children, one of which accounted for almost two-fifths (39%) of those in the study. However, it may also reflect the types of families in these areas for whom special guardianship was providing a suitable option. Adoptive placements for children from minority ethnic backgrounds are known to be harder to find (Lowe *et al*, 2002; Thoburn, 2002; Selwyn and Wijedasa, 2009) and some minority ethnic communities may find adoption difficult for cultural or religious reasons.

As we saw in Chapter 3, policy interviews in one area that had experienced a higher take-up by minority ethnic carers suggested that there was evidence that special guardianship was proving attractive to some relative carers. In these areas, there was also some evidence of these communities being targeted by children's services in order to promote take-up by introducing same-language lead officers and drop-in surgeries.

Consistent with findings from the policy interviews, however, there was limited survey evidence of special guardianship being used for unaccompanied asylum-seeking children in these local authorities. Only three children included in the survey sample had first come to the UK as asylum-seeking children. They were part of a sibling group, comprising 14-year-old twins and a younger brother. Children's services had placed these children with an adult cousin, their only family member in the UK, who had then made an application for special guardianship.

Age

The guidance and regulations suggest that special guardianship may provide security and permanence for older children for whom adoption may not be possible, appropriate or desired (Department for Education and Skills, 2005). Research indicates that the likelihood of finding an adoptive placement for a child diminishes with age (Lowe *et al*, 2002; Thoburn, 2002; Sinclair *et al*, 2007). Children six years old and over are less likely to be placed for adoption than younger children and it has been estimated that the odds of children not being adopted may increase by up to 1.8 times for each additional year they are looked after (Selwyn *et al*,

2006). Given this, it would seem that special guardianship could provide an appropriate permanence option for older children where the chances of adoption are receding. This may also be the case for older children and adolescents who are settled in long-term foster care and where they are reluctant to sever ties with their birth family.

With these points in mind it would appear that the children in our sample were quite young. The average age of children at the point they joined the study was 6.8 years of age. As Table 4.2 indicates, children ranged from babies of less than one year old through to young people aged 16. Less than a third (27%) of the sample, however, was aged between 10 and 16 years.

Table 4.2
The age of children at entry to the study

Age group	Number	Percentage
0–2 years	23	19
3–5 years	33	28
6–9 years	32	27
10–13 years	20	17
14–16 years	12	10

Where cases had reached a court decision, over one-half (52%) involved children aged five years or under and one-fifth (20%) involved babies of one year or under at the date the order was made. Though surprisingly low, the ages of children in the study are consistent with findings from other recent research on special guardianship, which found that 53 per cent of orders had been awarded for children under the age of five (Hall, 2008).

The age of the children for whom special guardianship is granted raises a number of wider issues. There are policy implications arising from the take-up of special guardianship and its potential impact on other permanence options, such as adoption. It is certainly possible that, for our sample at least, it may have been used for a group of younger children for whom adoption might still have been an option. The long-term nature of these permanence decisions also bears considerable similarity to those taken in adoption cases and should, therefore, be taken with the same degree of care. The age of the children also carries implications for services and resources, with the potential need for longer-term support for families who may need additional help to care for very young children or who may need to revisit services for support as the child grows older.

Health, disability and behavioural difficulties

Overall, children in the sample appeared relatively free of chronic health problems or physical, sensory or learning impairments. Just over four-fifths of the children (84%) were described as being in 'very good health'. As shown in Table 4.3, around one in eight children had learning disabilities. This included at least five cases where a diagnosis of autistic spectrum disorder had been made. Other difficulties were also identified, including ADHD, speech and language delay, dyspraxia and one child whose disability was linked to foetal alcohol syndrome. Chronic physical health problems affected only a minority of cases (four per cent) and included kidney problems and eczema. Four children in the sample were described by their carers as having a physical disability and here conditions included cerebral palsy and mobility problems.

Table 4.3
Child's health and disability

	Number (n = 120)	Percentage
Mental health problem	2	2
Physical disability	4	3
Chronic physical health problem	5	4
Learning disability	15	13

For the minority who did have health problems or impairments (21 in total), most (86%) were reported as having difficulties in only one of the above categories. However, three children had multiple difficulties.

Although there was very little evidence of mental health problems amongst these children, it is important to bear in mind that the majority were still very young children and there is evidence that mental health, emotional or behavioural difficulties may not emerge, or be reported, until children reach adolescence (Meltzer *et al*, 2000).

Table 4.4
Children's emotional and behavioural difficulties

	Number	*Percentage**
Serious problems	5	5
Moderate problems	13	12
Few problems	51	48
No problems	38	36
Total	**107**	**101**

* Percentage column does not total 100% due to rounding.

Despite the young age of the children, however, there was evidence that some had emotional and behavioural problems. Carers and social workers were asked to rate the child's emotional and behavioural development on a scale of 1 (serious problems) to 4 (no problems). The findings from carers and social workers were merged to maximise the data available for analysis. Where both sources of data were available for a particular case, the views of carers were given priority, since they had day-to-day care of the children concerned.

The findings, presented in Table 4.4, show that some problems were reported for around two-thirds of the children, although the proportion with serious difficulties was very small (five per cent). As we will see further in Chapter 8, the level of emotional and behavioural difficulties reported was lower than was the case for children in other forms of permanent placement, especially for children in long-term foster care or for those adopted by strangers. However, it is important to bear in mind that these children were still younger than those in other permanent placements at the point of follow-up.

Around one in seven of the children (14%) had a statement of educational need, rising to 19 per cent of those aged five or over and therefore likely to be at school.[26] This appears to be high in comparison to

---

[26] The statutory school starting age for children in the UK is the term after a child's fifth birthday. However, in England and Wales it is common practice to admit children to reception at the start of the year in which they will turn five; so many children will start school at the age of four. We have used five years of age as the starting point here.

recent national statistics, which report that 2.8 per cent of all school pupils had a statement (Department for Education and Skills, 2008). However, it is perhaps more broadly representative of groups of vulnerable children and young people, including those looked after in public care, for whom research shows that around one-quarter have been statemented (Berridge *et al*, 2002; Biehal, 2005). Overall, however, most (72%) of the children were rated by their carer and/or social worker to be doing quite well (38%) or very well (34%) at school.

Carer characteristics

Information gathered from carers and social workers allowed us to explore the characteristics of the 81 carers in the study who had applied for a special guardianship order.[27] The majority of primary carers were female (89%). Most, however, were part of a couple as only one-fifth of the sample (21%) indicated that they were not living with a partner. All of these lone carers were female.

There was a correlation between the ethnicity of the child and the carer, reflecting the high proportion of kinship carers seeking special guardianship.[28] Children living with relative carers were far more likely to match their carers' ethnicity (92%) than were those living with unrelated foster carers (57%).[29]

As shown in Table 4.5, the majority (60%) of carers described themselves as White and almost one-third (30%) as Black or Black British. The only apparent difference between carer and child's ethnicity was in relation to those children described as White and Black Caribbean/ African (13 per cent of children compared to three per cent of carers). This was apparent even after removing siblings from the analysis. Further analysis showed that two-thirds of these children were being cared for by Black/Black British carers and one-third by White carers.

---

[27] In a number of cases, information was received only from a carer or social worker questionnaire rather than both. We therefore do not have full data for all 81 carers.

[28] Fisher's Exact Test p<0.001.

[29] Fisher's Exact Test p<0.001.

Table 4.5
Carer's ethnic origin

Ethnic group	Number	Percentage*
White	46	60
Black or Black British	23	30
Asian	3	4
White and Black Caribbean/African	2	3
Chinese	1	1
Other ethnic group	2	3
Total	**77**	**101**

* Percentage column does not total 100% due to rounding.

Carers ranged in age from 22 to 70 years old, though the age distribution was skewed towards the higher end of the range. Although the average age for the sample was 49 years old, most (86%) were 40 years or over and almost half (47%) of the group were aged between 50 and 70 years at the time of data collection.

The relatively advanced age of carers stands out against the young ages of the children. Indeed, many of those carers of 50 and above were caring for very young children (75 per cent below the age of nine) with one-half of the carers aged over 60 having applied to become the special guardian of a child of eight years or under. In such circumstances, a scenario in which some carers would be in their mid-70s by the time the child reached 18 is quite possible. These findings reflect the high proportion of carers who were grandparents.

Nonetheless, this does raise several issues. The age gap between carers and their children presents questions around the longevity of these placements, both in terms of life expectancy for older carers and in terms of their ability and capacity, as they age, to care for young children or indeed to parent teenagers. This brings with it implications for the support, both formal and informal, that might be required currently and into the future to sustain the special guardianship relationship, and for an alternative future care plan for the child to be considered at the assessment stage in case one becomes necessary.

Some carers who had taken on the care of a very young child talked about the challenges this had brought. An aunt, who had become the special guardian of a baby aged two months, commented on the "culture shock" of caring for a baby:

> The first four months I thought I was going crazy, you know, I just didn't get any sleep . . . I went off sick [from work] to settle the baby in. I could not have coped. The first four months were the worst, suffering from sleep deprivation. She is hard work and, at the moment, she's just going through that . . . screaming for everything and crying endlessly.

A grandparent had also found that caring for two small children was particularly tiring and partially attributed that to her age:

> We've had her from being two days old and him from birth. It is hard work, very hard work . . . probably because I'm getting older, it's much harder.

Child and carer relationship

Most of the children (85%) were living with relatives. Table 4.6 shows the range of extended family members that were making use of the special guardianship option to care for a young relative. Kin applicants included older siblings, other relatives, such as cousins and great-aunts and, in one-fifth of cases (21%), aunts and uncles. Grandparents, however, were the most common applicants, accounting for just over half (53%) of the special guardianship cases in our local authorities.

Most grandparents were over 50 years of age, though the group included some relatively young grandparents who were in their early forties and two step-grandparents in their mid-30s. Most were living with partners, though one-quarter of the grandparent group consisted of grand-mothers living in lone carer households. The prominence of grandparents in our sample reflects recent research on kinship care, which suggests that grandparents are almost twice as likely as other relatives to take on the care of a young family member (Hunt *et al*, 2008). It is also consistent with Hall's study in which grandparents accounted for 68 per cent of the special guardians in the study (Hall, 2008).

Table 4.6
Children's relationship to their carers (n=120)

Relationship	Number	Percentage	Percentage of total sample
Friends and family	**104**		**87**
Grandparent	63	60	53
Aunt/uncle	25	24	21
Brother/sister	6	6	5
Other relative	8	8	6
Family friend	1	1	1
Other relationship	1	1	1
Unrelated foster carer	**16**		**13**
Total	**120**		**100**

Unrelated foster carers only accounted for a small minority (13%) of the cases. All but three were couples and they had been caring for the child for whom they had applied to become a special guardian for between two and nine years. Other applicants included a family friend and the adoptive parents of a child's older siblings.

These findings show that, in our local authorities at least, special guardianship was being used far more widely amongst kinship carers than unrelated foster carers. This is consistent with the findings discussed in Chapter 3, and suggests an apparent reluctance amongst foster carers to experience the change in their status and circumstances that would accompany a switch to special guardianship. Concerns centred on the uncertainty of how special guardianship may impact on a foster carer's financial situation together with the removal of the wider support they receive as the carer of a looked after child, and these were echoed in the views of one senior manager:

Special guardianship has been mentioned at looked after child reviews but foster carers have seemed reluctant, it's a new procedure, not fully established and maybe not enough support . . . financial and support packages are unclear. (Senior manager)

Related to this is the idea that some foster carers may feel that removing their child from the care system may deny the child some of the additional support they would receive as a looked after child. One local authority manager noted that current changes in support for looked after children, particularly around education provision (for example, priority access to school places, access to educational equipment, bursary for going to university) and the support available to young people leaving care (access to financial support and help with finding accommodation, education, employment and training) may adversely affect those leaving the care system for special guardianship:[30]

> *Some carers are reluctant because ... a child with special guardian-ship is no longer a looked after child ... what does this mean for support? One set of carers were put off because the educational support would be lost with a special guardianship order.* (Senior manager)

Wider organisational factors related to the retention of foster carers may also mean that some local authorities or fostering agencies may be reluc-tant to encourage their foster carers to move toward special guardianship. However, this seems less convincing, given the long-term financial advantages to services of removing a child and carer from the care system and because there is no reason why a special guardianship carer could not remain a foster carer for another child, as was the case with some of the carers in this study.

The fact that so many grandparents had taken on the care of a child emphasises the very important role that they play in family life. Grand-parents can and do play a significant part in the care of their grand-children generally (Clarke and Cains, 2001; Wheelock and Jones, 2002; Gray, 2005). In many cases, this involves providing or supplementing child care where children remain with their parents. Grandparents who become full-time carers of children, however, often struggle with a

---

[30] The Children and Young Persons Act 2008 extends and enhances the support for young people in and leaving care.

number of issues, which, whilst characteristic of kinship care, will also carry implications for special guardianship.

Taking on the care of a grandchild may not always be a completely free choice. Kinship carers can feel obligated or driven by a desire to prevent the child being removed from the family network. Several grandparents in our study commented that revisiting the role of "parent" was not something they had envisaged at this stage of their lives and whilst they did not regret the decision to care for their grandchild, their own life plans had been altered or put on hold. Grandparents as carers may also prompt some concerns amongst social workers about the adequacy of their parenting skills, either through ability or material circumstances. Indeed, Farmer and Moyers (2008) reported that kinship carers struggled to cope with children in their care more often than was the case for unrelated foster carers. Though all special guardianship applicants should be properly assessed with respect to their capacity to provide good-quality care, there remains the concern that some of these carers may have had shortcomings when parenting their own children and therefore may subsequently run into difficulties as children reach, as one social worker described it, 'that tricky teenager stage'. A few carers themselves expressed some anxiety over their ability to protect their grandchildren as they enter the teenage years. One grandmother's anxiety about the future for her grandchild was rooted in the experience of her own children and, by implication, in her sense of responsibility for not being able to prevent or control their growing dependence on drugs and alcohol:

> *I hope she don't go down same path as them, you know . . . Look what they've done with their lives . . . it's so sad. So I want better for her and I'll do my best, that's all I can do, do my best.*

Where were the children living before moving to their special guardianship household?

In order to understand the children's journeys towards special guardianship, information was collected about aspects of their backgrounds and family histories and of their past involvement with children's services.

Most (74%) of the children were already living with the carer who had subsequently applied to become their special guardian, whether on a *formal* or *informal* basis.[31]

As Table 4.7 shows, in nearly two-thirds (61%) of cases, this was a relative, many of whom were looking after the child on a "formal" basis (48%). Fifteen children (13%) were being looked after by an unrelated foster carer who had subsequently applied to become the child's special guardian.

Table 4.7
Type of placement prior to special guardianship application

	Number	*Percentage*
Living with the special guardianship carer prior to application/order:		
Kinship (formal)	58	48
Kinship (informal)	16	13
Unrelated foster carer	15	13
Living with a non-special guardianship carer prior to application/order:		
Unrelated foster carer	29	24
Birth parents	2	2
Total	**120**	**100**

In just over one-quarter (26%) of cases, children had not been living with the carer who had applied for special guardianship. With the exception of two children who had been living with birth parents while their grandparents made an application, all were living with an unrelated foster carer (24%) who was caring for the child on a care order whilst a family member applied for a special guardianship order.

---

[31] Carers looking after the child on a "formal" basis included those where a legal order (a full care order, interim care order or residence order) was in place. Where there was no evidence of an order, carers were described as caring for a child on an "informal" basis.

The special guardianship household

Among those children who were living with their special guardianship carers at the time of data collection, two-thirds (65%) had been living there for two or more years.[32] The average length of stay for the sample as a whole was three years, but the duration ranged from three months to 11 years. Overall, most children therefore appeared quite well settled with their carers before the decision was made to apply for special guardianship.

The composition of the household was frequently quite complex for both those living with unrelated foster carers and those living with relatives. Almost one-third (32%) of the children were living with their siblings. Many were also living with other unrelated children, including children who were fostered or subject to residence orders. Some households included the carer's birth children, some of whom, in kinship households, were the young aunts or uncles of the special guardianship child. This could lead to quite interesting and complicated family scenarios, as demonstrated by one-year-old Jonathan's situation. Here, the household comprised the maternal grandfather and his new partner together with their baby daughter, to be known as Jonathan's sister (though in actual fact his aunt) and the partner's 12-year-old son, to be known as Jonathan's brother, although technically his step-uncle. Such family circumstances where relationships are renegotiated and often blurred are not uncommon in kinship care settings.

Care history and past involvement with children's services

As we have seen, many of the children had been subject to a legal order. The survey provided information on children's past involvement with children's services and on whether plans for adoption had figured in earlier plans for permanence.

---

[32] At the point of data collection, only six children had not yet moved to live with their prospective special guardians. These cases were excluded from this analysis.

Child's care status

As Table 4.8 indicates, almost three-quarters of the children (70%) were looked after at the time of the special guardianship application. Over one-half of these cases (59%) had been granted a special guardianship order by the time data collection took place and had, therefore, subsequently left the care system. In these cases, special guardianship was being used as an exit strategy from the system. The fact that such a high proportion had been looked after also points to the troubled family backgrounds of these children and to the services that might be required to help carers meet their needs successfully.

Table 4.8
Care status immediately prior to application/order

Care status	Number	Percentage
Looked after:		
Unrelated foster care	44	37
Kinship foster care	40	33
Not looked after:		
Kinship – residence order	19	16
Kinship – no order	17	14
Total	**120**	**100**

Just under one-third (30%) of children had not been looked after at the time of application. All were living with relatives, some on residence orders and others informally, including two who were living with birth parents.

Past involvement with children's services

Most of the children were reported by social workers to have had a history of contact with children's services and many had been looked after for several years. Since this information was only requested from social workers, it is not available for all cases (n = 86) and may therefore under-estimate the extent of past professional involvement in the lives of these children.

The vast majority of these children had been known to children's services in the past (95%). Involvement had often been long standing: for more than two years in two-fifths of cases (43%) and five years or more in a quarter. The nature of social work involvement varied. In some instances, the focus of attention had been the individual child. In others, the child was known through broader preventive support provided to the family or through concerns about the welfare of siblings. More than two-fifths of these children (44%) had been placed on the Child Protection Register and an equal number had been in receipt of family support services.

Most of these children had been subject to a range of legal orders in the past, including interim care orders (71%), full care orders (31%), emergency protection orders (24%), supervision orders (6%) or residence orders (5%). Only in one in nine cases (11%) was there no evidence of a past legal order. Across the sample as a whole, almost three-quarters of the children (73%) had been looked after at some stage.

In interviews, some carers discussed the effects of movement and disruption during these early phases of children's lives and their implications for children's sense of permanence and stability, difficulties that they hoped would be resolved through special guardianship:

[He] was removed from his parents on an emergency protection order at 16 months. He was in care for about eight months of his life before he came here on a care order. He had two other sets of foster carers in that time . . . so he had a lot of moves for such a young baby and it's affected him . . . Emotionally he's behind his years, emotionally [he is] very unstable [especially] if anything changes . . . He likes routine. (Great-aunt, child now six years old)

Some relatives talked about having had months of conflict between themselves and children's services when a child had been placed with unrelated foster carers, even though family members were willing to care for the child. In some cases, children had moved three or four times before finally being placed with the relative who became their special guardian:

It was bad to think that [her social worker] didn't want her to come and stay with me. Yet she placed her with strangers . . . in a place where there were a lot of problems . . . So she was moved again from that one . . . to another foster carer . . . We are her family now that she is here with me. (Grandmother, child now eight years old)

Consistent with information provided by practitioners through policy interviews, special guardianship was therefore being used primarily for children in the looked after system (the majority) or for children on the edge of care. Most of these children were already in the care of relatives and only a minority (37%) had been living with unrelated foster carers immediately prior to the special guardianship placement. Only a very small minority of cases involved families not previously known to children's services. This perhaps helps to explain why the policy interviews revealed little knowledge amongst social work managers about these "private" applications (see Chapter 3).

Plans for adoption

In a sizeable minority of cases (28%), special guardianship had been awarded for children for whom adoption had been considered at some stage in the care plan. Not surprisingly, virtually all of these children (91%) had been looked after, with almost two-thirds (63%) living with an unrelated foster carer and just 29 per cent living with a kinship foster carer. The remaining two cases were living with relatives, one on a residence order and the other informally.

It is not possible to explore from these data whether the intention was to have the children adopted by relatives or by strangers, though none of the current carers indicated that the child had been placed with them for adoption. We were also unable to identify how many of these cases had been awarded a special guardianship order in the course of care or adoption proceedings. However, social workers were asked to indicate why the plan for adoption had changed.

In some cases, family members had come forward during the course of care or adoption proceedings to prevent the child being placed outside the family. Even where there was a strong desire to care for the child long term within the family, adoption by a family member was sometimes considered not suitable or not feasible by children's services or by the family themselves. Explanations focused on the complications that might be created in the balance of family relationships or in relationships with other children in the household, where some were fostered and others were on residence orders. In these circumstances, adoption could create divisions between children or between carers and birth parents. Considerations also included overt opposition by birth parents to adoption and the identification of special guardianship as a more amenable option. In the case of some older children, retention of a positive link with birth parents was paramount over the additional security that might accrue through adoption.

> Plans were changed when the maternal aunt came forward as a guardian during care/adoption proceedings.

> Adoption was considered but not pursued as this was not entirely appropriate due to the fact of it altering the relationship with the birth family.

> Plans were changed due to guardian having two other children on residence orders. They felt they could not offer adoption to the four siblings as the other two children in her care could not be adopted.

> I felt that the birth mother's attachment to child and vice versa was strong and needed to be maintained. Also I thought it might create difficulties within the family as birth mother strongly opposed adoption and had support from family.

There was little evidence of plans for adoption being altered in light of an unsuccessful attempt to find a suitable adoptive family or through placement breakdown. Only one social worker indicated that the plan for the child had changed because a suitable adopter could not be found and, in one further case, an adoptive placement had been found but had broken down after 18 months. Similarly, there was only one indication that a plan to adopt had been changed as a result of cultural objection.

This child was from a Traveller community with a very specific cultural heritage ... The Travelling community made it clear that they do not agree with adoption, although they felt the child could not return to the birth parents and therefore a special guardianship order appeared to suit this scenario.

Arrival stories: reasons for placement

Given what is known about the histories of these children, it is not surprising to find that the reasons for their separation from birth parents and for their eventual arrival in a special guardianship household bear considerable similarity to those of other children in the looked after system. Indeed, two-thirds of these children (64 per cent) had been placed with their current carers by the local authority concerned.

Table 4.9 provides a breakdown of the background factors that led to the children living with their current carers. Social workers and carers were asked to indicate which of a list of possible factors were relevant to the child in question. Other non-listed factors could also be written into the questionnaire. Where information was provided by both the social worker and carer in a particular case, if either recorded that a particular factor existed then this information was included. As such, the findings may slightly inflate the range of reasons underpinning separation from birth parents. They also have to be understood as overlapping reasons underpinning both separation and placement, since respondents were asked to indicate all factors that applied.

The picture that emerges is one in which there had been quite serious concerns about the actual or potential maltreatment of children. In two-thirds of cases, there was evident concern about the child's safety with their birth parent(s) and in two-fifths of cases, about their failure to thrive. If these are combined and taken together as a proxy measure for maltreatment, this was evident for over two-thirds of children (68%) in the study. As we have seen, more than two-thirds (70%) had been removed from the care of their parents and were living in public care prior to their current placement and these factors would have been uppermost in the minds of social workers when making those decisions. Behind this, there is a story of significant minorities of parents grappling with alcohol or drug

Table 4.9
Background factors leading to placement

Reasons	Number	Percentage
Parent unable to care:		
Death of child's parent	9	8
Parent unable to care due to physical health/disability	9	8
Parent unable to care – mental health problem	33	28
Absent parent	2	2
Parent problems:		
Parent unable to care – substance misuse	40	33
Domestic violence in family home*	14	12
Child concerns:		
Risk to safety of child	80	67
Child's failure to thrive	49	41
Child–parent relationship breakdown	4	3
Parent unable to manage child's behaviour	1	1
Mutual obligations:		
Carer – family obligation*	18	15
Child's wish to live with guardian	14	12

* These questions were not included in the original questionnaires, but have been included here because of the number of responses of this type from carers. They are therefore very likely to underestimate the extent of these background factors, perhaps especially the influence of family obligations.

dependency, mental health problems and, to a lesser extent, with their physical health and disabilities. There is also evidence of unreliable, sometimes violent, relationships with partners that is likely to be underestimated in this dataset. These background factors are broadly consistent with those found for children entering the looked after system more generally (Gibbs *et al*, 2005).

For a small number of children (8%), placement had been precipitated by the death of a parent. In one instance, the death of a lone parent had led the grandmother to foster and then become special guardian for a sibling group of four young children. In another, a short-term unrelated foster carer became special guardian to a sibling group of four children when their birth mother died and no other family members were found to be willing to take the children.

Although it was not surprising to find that only a minority of children were reported as having wanted to live with their carers at this time, there was some evidence of the mutual obligations that bind many families together. Around one in seven carers wrote on the questionnaire that a motivating factor had been to keep the children within the family network – *'because s/he is family'*. No doubt, if this option had been available to all carers, the proportion responding would have been higher.

In order to provide some greater depth to the arrival stories of children, this chapter concludes with a small number of case studies that draw together some of these background factors in a more integrated manner.

Case study
Sachin – living with his kinship foster carers who became his special guardians

Sachin had lived with his birth parents and two younger siblings until the age of five. His mother had a history of mental illness, which had involved hospitalisation on several occasions. All three children were known to children's services and were on the Child Protection Register due to concerns over their safety. The children had suffered injuries throughout their early years, though it was not clear whether these were inflicted by the mother or were accidents due to neglect and poor parenting. Sachin was finally removed from his parents' care after his mother inflicted serious injuries. Both the birth mother and father, who had failed to seek medical assistance for his child, received a custodial sentence and the younger siblings were placed with a relative. On leaving hospital, Sachin was placed with a series of unrelated foster carers until his uncle and aunt applied to care for him and his siblings. Eventually he was placed with them on an interim care order. Children's services decided that the children could not return to the parents. Sachin's uncle initially applied for a residence order but was subsequently advised to seek special guardianship. The family felt this would provide a secure option and the order was granted two years after the child had moved in with them.

Case study
Lucy – living with an unrelated foster carer who became her special guardian
Lucy, along with her younger half-siblings, had lived with her birth mother until the age of eight. Her father had left the household and her mother was living with a new partner. The household was extremely volatile with frequent incidents of domestic violence between the mother and stepfather, which were witnessed by the children. The children had been known to children's services for several years and were on the Child Protection Register for abuse and neglect. Further investigations revealed evidence that the children were victims of physical abuse inflicted by their mother, and that Lucy had been sexually abused by a male relative. The children were removed from the household and placed on an emergency protection order with unrelated foster carers. They were later placed on a full care order with another foster carer, who went on to apply for special guardianship for the sibling group. The carer considered this a more appropriate and equitable option than adoption as she was also caring for two other unrelated children on a residence order as well as the four siblings. The siblings' history of abuse and neglect had impacted upon their emotional and physical development and the carer noted evidence of learning disabilities and emotional and behavioural difficulties. However, she felt the children had adapted well to their new family and were 'much happier'. Lucy's social worker commented on the importance of special guardianship for her: 'She needed a stable environment to live and grow and remaining with these carers has prevented her being shipped around the authority's foster carers.'

Case study
Martin – living with a relative who became his special guardian
Martin had lived with his mother, a lone carer, together with his older siblings until he was seven. He had not been in care in the past. However, it subsequently became apparent that there had been a long

history of neglect within the family. His early childhood had been particularly harrowing, having discovered the body of a relative who had died. Martin had also been subjected to violence and physical abuse by an older sibling. His special guardian described his childhood as being 'neglectful and cruel': 'They weren't being looked after, just neglected and left in front of the television. He wasn't talked to, just completely neglected.' His mother received a custodial sentence for unrelated offences and Martin was taken in by his aunt on an informal basis. Children's services decided that the child could not be returned to his birth mother, so Martin's aunt began proceedings to obtain a residence order. During court proceedings, she was advised that special guardianship would offer greater security and permanence. This was supported by his birth parents and was awarded 18 months later.

Summary

- Information on the characteristics of the children and carers who had applied for special guardianship was available for 120 children and 81 carers. Half of the cases involved applications for a single child. The remaining cases were part of a sibling group. In all, there were 21 sibling groups in the study.
- The profiles of the children and carers suggest that special guardianship is being used more widely than might have been envisaged by government, the majority of cases involving relative carers looking after younger children from mainly troubled backgrounds.
- A similar number of boys and girls were subject to special guardianship applications across our local authorities. The sample included a high proportion of minority ethnic children (45%), which may reflect the local authority areas involved rather than the type of carers applying for special guardianship.
- Most children were relatively young. The majority (52%) were aged five years or under and 20 per cent were under one year of age at the time the order was made. This carries policy and practice implications around take-up and the impact on other permanence options and resources, given the potential need for longer-term support.

- Most applicants were relative carers (85%) and only one in seven (13%) applications came from unrelated foster carers. Almost half (47%) of the carers in the study were aged between 50 and 70 years of age, reflecting the high proportion of grandparents (53%) making applications.
- Three-quarters of children had already been living with their carer for some time prior to the application. Most had been living with kin carers either formally (care order or residence order – 48%) or informally (13%) and a further 13 per cent of children had been living with unrelated foster carers who had subsequently applied to become the children's special guardians.
- The majority (73%) of children had been in public care. Just under half of these (45%) had been looked after by kinship foster carers and the remainder had been in unrelated foster carer. Only one-third (34%) of unrelated foster carers had applied to become the special guardian of the child. At the point of data collection, 59 per cent of those looked after had been awarded special guardianship and had therefore exited the care system.
- Many children had complex and troubled family histories. For most children (68%), there had been concerns about maltreatment and many had come from very difficult family circumstances, character-ised by parental substance misuse, mental health problems and, perhaps to a lesser degree, domestic violence.
- The characteristics of this special guardianship sample raise a number of practice and resource issues for service providers. If special guard-ianship is to prove to be a successful permanence option for children, then factors such as the age profile of children and, to a degree, their carers, their troubled family backgrounds, and the continuing needs that may arise from these point to the likelihood that a support infra-structure (mainstream or specialist) will be required to support the endeavour of these families.

5 Application, assessment, preparation and the court hearing

In the previous chapter we looked at the difficulties experienced by children and their families and explored the reasons why the children were living away from their birth parents. This chapter considers important aspects of the journey towards special guardianship. It considers how the applications for special guardianship came about and the factors that motivated carers to apply, and charts their experiences up to the final court hearing.

Information on the application, assessment and court process was collected from carers for index children only, so for most areas we therefore have data for 51 cases. Some process information, however, was also collected on index cases from social workers. This has enabled us to draw upon some information for a larger number of cases.

The application

Prospective special guardians must give the responsible local authority[33] at least three months' notice of their intention to apply, unless given leave of the court to make an application in the context of existing family proceedings. If the court is considering making an order of its own motion, it must direct the local authority to prepare a report assessing the background and suitability of the applicants.[34]

Information on the application status of cases was available for 83 per cent of the sample (n = 100).[35] These cases were, however, at different

---

[33] If the application involves a looked after child, notice must be given to the responsible local authority. In all other cases, notice should be given to the local authority in which the carer lives.

[34] *Re S* [2007] EWCA Civ 54.

[35] We have missing data for 20 cases. These are all sibling cases for which we did not receive a social worker questionnaire. One option to maximise the data would have been to use data from the corresponding index sibling to infer the status of these cases. However, we decided against this as not all siblings were subject to the same special guardianship order. In some cases, a new application had been subsequently started for a child after an order had been granted for a sibling.

stages. Some carers were still in the application process (n = 24). The majority of cases (n = 75), however, had reached a court decision and, in all these cases, a special guardianship order had been granted. Just one kinship foster carer withdrew her application after data collection had started, due to concerns about the reduction in support she would receive if she had proceeded. As her social worker explained:

> *In this case the special guardianship application was withdrawn since she understood that children's services would pull out once an order was made. The grandmother wanted to retain the support of children's services because there were lots of other issues involved.*

Who initiated the application?

At the time of data collection, special guardianship was still a relatively new option and, as we will see further below, the information available to potential applicants was quite variable. Carers identified a number of different avenues for obtaining initial information, including social workers, solicitors, the courts, family support workers and children's guardians. A small number had first heard through their informal networks, or through helplines, voluntary agencies, publicly available literature or the internet. In some instances, the child's existing foster carer had suggested it to relatives.

Some carers had made an independent decision to apply (53%); others reported that they had been advised by professionals (47%). There was some association with the age of the child. Those who reported that they had made an independent choice to apply had tended to do so for older children.[36] In a context where most cases had arisen in the public law arena and concerned looked after children or children on the edge of care, this finding is noteworthy. It implies that carers were rather more likely to be advised or persuaded to seek special guardianship in cases concerning younger children, perhaps in the context of family proceedings. Some carers of young children reported that they had been seeking placement orders prior to adoption before being persuaded of the merits of special

---

[36] Mann-Whitney U Exact Test: p = 0.02; n = 35.

guardianship by social workers, solicitors or the courts. Of course, this may have been a more appropriate option for them, although there were some cases where carers had experienced a degree of coercion or felt that, as an option, it might be second best:

> *It was children's services' [decision]. We felt that it would be better to adopt her... At the time we didn't know anything about special guardianship.* (Grandmother, child aged 18 months)

> *We were not given a choice. We wanted to adopt. We were going to court and they said: 'What we're prepared to do is not give you the adoption. There's a new thing out... called special guardianship... We're prepared to do that'... and I wasn't happy with this but, in the end, we accepted special guardianship... because the baby was staying in care all this time.* (Aunt, child aged three)

> *Special guardianship was suggested to me by my supervising social worker. I'm still not sure if it's right for me. I'm worried about support, both financially and to meet his special needs.* (Unrelated foster carer, boy aged 14)

In cases where carers had initially been seeking a residence order, the advice or direction could, however, be welcome:

> *We applied for a residence order. Then my solicitor said a special guardianship order is coming out and it would be advisable for us to go for it rather than an adoption or residence order. So the court allowed us to change it to the guardianship order.* (Grandmother, boy aged nine)

Those who had chosen to apply had also often received advice from social workers or solicitors, who had raised it as a possible option amongst others. In these cases, carers had often sought out further information and weighed the evidence before making a formal approach:

> *It was mentioned by the social worker at a review meeting. Once I was*

clear about special guardianship and adoption, we chose special guardianship. (Aunt, former kinship foster carer of boy aged 16)

Information provided by social workers suggested that special guardianship had most commonly been discussed during planning or review meetings (50%), reflecting the high number of looked after children in the sample (see Table 5.1). However, they also reported that one in nine carers (11%) had been awarded an order during the course of other court proceedings. In all of these cases, the child was under seven years of age and most (71%) had been living with relatives on care or residence orders.

Table 5.1

How did the special guardianship application come to children's services' attention?

	Number	*Percentage*
Guardian gave notice	20	30
Court awarded special guardianship order	7	11
Looked after child planning or review meeting	33	50
Child in need/planning meeting	1	2
Other circumstances, for example, court gave leave to apply	5	7
Total	**66**	**100**

Reasons for applying

Carers were asked to indicate how important certain factors had been in their decision to apply for or accept a special guardianship order. As Table 5.2 shows, carers' main priorities were to provide their child with a legally secure permanent home and to be able to exercise greater parental control. These are very much in line with the intentions of special guardianship. Of almost equal importance was a desire to prevent the child being removed from the family network or to have them restored to it. Less significant, though still very important for over two-fifths of respondents, was the promise that special guardianship holds for financial or other services and support to help carers meet the needs of children.

Table 5.2
Factors identified as 'very important' in the decision to apply

Reasons for application	Very important	
	Number	Percentage
I wanted to provide a permanent and stable home for this child	51	100
I wanted to have more control over decisions affecting this child's life	45	88
I wanted to provide this child with greater legal security	42	82
I wanted to prevent this child being removed from my care in the future	42	82
I wanted to prevent this child from entering or remaining in care	39	76
I wanted this child to keep a link with his/her birth parent(s)	30	59
I hoped for some financial help from children's services to meet the needs of this child	23	45
I hoped for some ongoing support from children's services to meet the needs of this child	21	41
Other options for this child, such as adoption, were either not wanted or were not possible	19	37

Embarking upon the journey to special guardianship was therefore driven by a variety of personal motives and incentives. Information from the survey and case studies provided greater detail about the motivations of carers. Whilst a number of cross-cutting issues emerged, it was possible to draw out a number of key themes underpinning their decisions.

For some, special guardianship provided an attractive option. Some carers had opted for it because it gave them enhanced parental responsibility in comparison to residence orders:

> *With special guardianship it seems as if you do get more power. It was a more secure order for us to apply for rather than a residence order. It gave us a bigger share of parental responsibility.* (Great-aunt)

The enhanced strength of special guardianship could lead, as some commentators have noted, to it superseding residence orders as the private law order of choice (see also Hall, 2008). On this, time will tell.

Some carers preferred special guardianship as a permanence option rather than adoption. In circumstances where relationships with birth parents were more harmonious, where birth parents might be resistant to adoption or where relatives had assumed the care of children within the family, it was sometimes seen by carers as having a less disruptive effect on the balance of relationships:

> *I did not want to adopt my own grandchild. Adoption, well you don't want to do that type of thing . . . Remember this is family . . . So guardianship seemed to be a nicer way of going forward and [provided] a bit more control for us.* (Aunt)

Where parents might be resistant, special guardianship was sometimes seen as a quicker and easier route to achieving permanence. In one or two cases, it was perceived to be a potential stepping-stone to adoption:

> *I think it is quicker to go for the special guardianship than for adoption . . . That is what really done it. Because the process for adoption can pan out longer, especially if you get any parent opposing it . . . But myself and [child] talked about the special guardianship or adoption and he said, 'Which is the quickest way?' . . . I said, 'Special guardianship because, once it goes through, I've got the option to adopt later on'.* (Unrelated foster carer)

Keeping the child within the family was a strong motivation for kinship carers. This included a desire to prevent the child going into care or being adopted by strangers. Some carers had come forward at an early point in the assessment process. Others had arrived late on the scene during the course of care proceedings:

> *If I didn't do this we would not have seen her again as under-fives are adopted out by Social Services.* (Grandmother, child aged three)

In some cases, it also reflected the worry that sibling groups would eventually be separated:

[Children's Services] told us that the three boys would not be adopted together. The thought of that was what made up my mind to take on all three boys permanently. (Grandmother)

Kinship carers were generally driven by a strong sense of family duty to care for and raise young relatives. Some expressed the feeling that a family bond could better ensure the child a loving home and enable the child to feel rooted within the family network. Carers were also strongly motivated by a desire to provide a better life for the child and to make up for past disadvantages. Keeping children within the network would also help to preserve connections between children and their birth parents where these relationships were helpful:

He is our grandson and he should be with family who love and care about him. We're a close family and I realised that special guardianship was the best way of keeping him in the family. But at the same time I'm his legal guardian, but his mum will still have a major impact in his life. (Grandmother)

With special guardianship it would be permanent with her . . . It gives me a better option to start . . . rebuilding her life . . . She had that . . . disadvantage in the first six years. I can put it right by having her legally protected with the legal autonomy to raise her myself. (Grandmother)

Feelings of obligation and commitment to children within the network, however, often came at a high price:

I've got all my kids grown up. I was living on my own. I was working two jobs . . . having three holidays a year and I gave up the lot for [her]. [My family] supported me 'cos they knew what I was giving up and they knew I could not see my granddaughter go into care. (Grandmother)

In contrast to preventing separation from the child, other kinship carers were motivated by the desire to have looked after children returned to family settings or, for some kinship foster carers, to be free of social work involvement in their lives. In these scenarios, priority was given to the normalisation of family life, even though some appreciated the potential for renewed support and services, should they be needed:

> *I'm hoping to get special guardianship so they can leave the care system and live with me. Because I love my grandkids dearly and I know they feel the same. They should never have been put into foster care when I was willing to care for them from day one. [I want] more stability for [the] children, without asking if they can visit their friends or have sleepovers. The children also want it. It makes a lot of sense after all these years with the authorities coming in and out, different ones every five minutes, to get on and have a proper life, a proper family. Not being different in any way: stability, love, keeping safe, growing into young adults together.* (Former kinship foster carer)

As Table 5.2 indicated, the enhanced parental responsibility and legal security afforded through special guardianship was very attractive to carers. It provided a good degree of protection against future challenges by birth parents over the legitimacy of the placement and against them suddenly wanting the child returned. It also afforded carers greater autonomy in taking important decisions concerning the child's welfare:

> *This new guardianship order, it stands for more authority because I've got [them] until they're 18. There's no way on this earth that [birth parent] is going to get them back. I got reassurance, now they are here they aren't going anywhere.* (Grandmother)

> *With parental responsibility over the child I felt it important that I could make decisions for myself without the approval of others. I felt it was in the child's best interests, as I had looked after her from birth.* (Uncle)

Where birth parents retained a presence in the child's life, the order provided some boundaries for these relationships and appeared to provide the carer with a legal framework for exercising the deciding vote in negotiations with family members. This was particularly important where these relationships were conflicted, as was the case for a grandmother who had been awarded a special guardianship order by the courts against the wishes of the child's father:

Thank God special guardianship came along because my daughter and [the child's] dad are separated . . . and you're never going to get three people to agree. Obviously my daughter is of the opinion, 'I trust you, Mum, to make the right decision' but her dad isn't of that opinion. So at least we have something that backs us. The special guardianship seems to us an excellent thing because it does protect you . . . [and] . . . the child's not going to be constantly battled over.
(Grandmother)

Taking on the care of a child brings with it increased financial responsibility, so financial considerations were important. For many carers, however, the care of a child was paramount and several talked of financing costly court cases themselves and getting into debt through the additional expenses incurred by caring for the child or a sibling group and, in some instances, through carrying out costly but necessary home renovations to accommodate their enlarged family.

While there seemed to be a level of uncertainty as to what carers could expect in terms of the financial arrangements, there was evidence that carers had been encouraged to apply on the advice or belief that special guardianship could offer greater financial support than other options, such as residence orders. These considerations could be of particular importance to carers who would have to give up work to care for a very young child:

[My social worker advised me] to go for the one with the most money . . . and it was special guardianship, that's what I was having.
(Grandmother)

[My social worker] said you'll be eligible for help. Once it's done, if there is anything that [the child] will need or anything needs to be done to the home, there's some special help. (Grandmother)

The financial help as well, that swayed me [over a residence order]. They pay twice a year for us to [travel] to see his mum, so we get help that way. (Aunt)

Support to apply for special guardianship

Table 5.3 shows the range of formal and informal sources of advice, information and guidance that carers relied upon once they had decided to make an application. Social workers, legal professionals and children's guardians were very much to the fore, reflecting the high proportion of looked after children in the sample and of those already involved in public law proceedings.

Table 5.3
Sources of advice in relation to the special guardianship application (n = 51)[37]

	Percentage
Social worker (children's services)	77
Solicitor/legal advice centre	55
CAFCASS worker (children's guardian)	35
Court official (during care, adoption or other proceedings)	15
Social worker (from another agency)	10
Health professional (GP, health visitor, mental health service)	10
Foster/residential carer	4
Family support worker	6
Members of your family or child's family	28
Friends	6
No one, I decided by myself	10

---

[37] Carers were asked to indicate all the categories that applied. Many received advice from a wide range of sources.

Families and friends had also been influential in the decision-making process for around one-third (34% in total) of carers. This included members of the child's wider family, the carer's family and, in some cases, birth parents themselves:

> *My family have always been supportive. The first couple of meetings at the court, [the child's] birth mum actually came with me and gave her consent.* (Maternal grandmother)

> *I must say both mum and dad are very [supportive]. Everything we said, they said 'fine'. I think because the option was basically [social services] were going to take [the child] away, so he was either going to stay with me or he was going to a foster home and they didn't want that.* (Aunt)

Overall, two-thirds of carers (67%) reported that they had received enough advice and support to make the 'right' decision and a further one in seven (14%) felt they had been helped 'to some degree'. However, 18 per cent said they had not received sufficient advice and more than one-quarter (28%) indicated that they would have liked more information. In particular, carers lacked information about the financial assistance and legal help that might be available, the stages involved in the process, how special guardianship differed in practice from other orders, and how these options would affect them personally. Some would have appreciated more written information in the form of accessible booklets or leaflets that set out their entitlements clearly across the different permanence options.

To some extent, the lack of information and guidance was associated with the relatively recent introduction of special guardianship. Indeed, the study included some carers who were amongst the first applicants in their local authorities. Consequently, some commented on a lack of knowledge and information generally amongst professionals and agencies, including social work and legal services. Furthermore, as we saw in Chapter 3, the new provisions had been implemented unevenly across the eight local authorities. It is therefore likely that a greater store of information (and publications) were available in some areas than in others:

We were one of the first and it was a bit hit-and-miss really. No one knew what they were doing. [The social worker] told us to get some independent legal advice and I rang round several local solicitors and they were very hazy about special guardianship, so in the end we didn't bother to take . . . legal advice. (Unrelated foster carer)

Consequently, many carers talked about navigating their way through the early stages of application by searching out their own information from books, organisations and websites. The internet had proved a useful resource to a number of carers in the study:

Social services brought it up, but . . . we didn't know what it meant or implied, so the information that we found out was by digging on the internet and talking to other people in similar situations. Not many . . . It's not until it happens that you find a network, but we were trying to glean information. (Grandmother)

Mainstream agencies, such as health and education, were also frequently found to be ill-informed. One special guardian found herself having to explain her new status to teachers and medical professionals:

I don't think it's been explained to schools. I did actually have to give a copy of my paperwork on special guardianship to the school because they just said: 'What's special guardianship?' To be honest, even doctors, when you take the child to the hospital, they don't even understand. (Unrelated foster carer)

The provision of clear and accurate information and guidance to carers considering special guardianship is crucial to ensure they are able to make an informed decision about whether it is the best option for them and their child. As we have seen, the majority of applicants felt that, overall, they had managed to access enough information and support to make the decision to apply. However, there clearly remains a gap in available guidance and information. Whether this is an effect of the early days of implementation or the extent to which local authorities have embraced it as an option remains to be seen. Nevertheless, there is a need to ensure that all relevant agencies and services are aware of special guardianship and the legal rights that it confers on carers. This might be addressed through the development of detailed and standardised practice guidance and training for all relevant professionals.

The assessment process and court report

The local authority will be made aware of a carer's application for special guardianship through a social worker, the legal services department, a solicitor acting on behalf of the applicant or by the courts. On receiving notice of a carer's intention to apply, the local authority, or someone appointed on their behalf,[38] must make an assessment of the child, family and carer's circumstances and then submit a report to the court on the carer's suitability to be a special guardian, along with any other relevant information. In all cases, the court must have received this report from the local authority before it can grant a special guardianship order (Department for Education and Skills, 2005).[39]

Preparation of the report involves a social worker visiting the carer and, where possible, the child and their birth parents to carry out a Regulation 21 assessment to gather relevant information. How the assessment should be conducted is not prescribed in regulations, although the guidance encourages use of the *Framework for Assessment of Children in Need and Their Families* (Department for Education and Skills, 2005; Department of Health, 2000b). All but three of the carers reported that they had met with a social worker to discuss these issues. Where this had not happened, assessments had been conducted by an independent agency or by a support worker from a kinship team in collaboration with a social worker.

Social workers reported that court reports had been prepared for all but six per cent of cases at the time of data collection. Those remaining were at an earlier stage in the process. However, there were a few instances where special guardianship orders had been awarded by the

---

[38] The local authority can make arrangements for this investigation to be carried out by a suitably qualified and experienced professional on its behalf.

[39] *Re S* [2007] EWCA Civ 54.

courts without a Regulation 21 report having been prepared. In these scenarios, the court had generally made the order of its own motion when local authorities had been seeking a different outcome – for example, kinship foster care or adoption – and had relied on assessments prepared for these:

There was no report done. It was supposed to be done, but in [the local authority's] defence it was a very tricky court case. Obviously the parents wanted [the child] back. The [Children's] Guardian wanted her adopted. We had a social worker come round and do a foster assessment, so she gave that evidence in court . . . The judge overruled everybody and ordered her to us on [a special guardianship order]. (Grandmother)

What did assessments cover?

The regulations state that, in preparing the court report, information should be gathered in the following areas (Department for Education and Skills, 2005):

- the child (family background, relationships and contact arrangements, culture, religion and race, educational and health needs);
- the child's family (details of birth parents and the child's siblings, including religion, culture, race, health and relationships);
- the child's and parents' wishes and feelings about special guardianship, where possible;
- the prospective special guardian (family composition and circumstances; parenting capacity; health; attitude in relation to child's and parent's wishes with respect to his/her religious and cultural upbringing; feelings about contact with birth parents and extended family; and reasons for applying for a special guardianship order);
- the local authority (details of any social work involvement, past or current, with the child and family; details of any special guardianship support services to be provided to the child, carer and the birth parents, or, if a decision not to provide such services, the reasons for this);

- an assessment of how a special guardianship order would meet the child's long-term needs as compared with other types of order.

The interviews with policy and practice professionals suggested some variations in the type and level of information collected. Some local authorities had tended to develop their own assessment tools based on the guidance, while others had adopted the Family Rights Group assessment template, which was being piloted at the time.[40]

However, the survey responses from carers and social workers suggested that assessments had provided fairly good coverage of the key areas. In most cases, assessments of need for support had been carried out simultaneously. In this chapter, we look specifically at the assessment of the carer and child. Support issues are covered in detail in Chapter 8.

Table 5.4 shows that, with respect to assessment on the background, suitability and motivation of applicants, most carers reported that these had been a focus of attention during the assessment. There was, as might be expected, some difference of opinion between carers and social workers. Overall, the vast majority of carers felt that the key areas had been covered during the assessment, even if not to their entire satisfaction. From the perspective of carers, slightly less attention had been given to their education and employment history and their financial and housing circumstances. These are important areas that ought to be considered carefully to ensure that carers are able to provide a financially secure environment for the child and that taking on special guardianship will not destabilise the family through financial hardship. Indeed, one carer noted that:

Since having the special guardianship order, we have had our home repossessed due to lack of funding. This has had an effect on my feelings about the whole thing. (Grandfather, caring for three young siblings)

---

[40] The Family Rights Group, in partnership with BAAF and the Fostering Network, has developed an assessment tool for assessment of family and friends carers. It is a three-stage assessment, depending on the assessment purpose. Taken together, the three sections provide the information that would be needed in a special guardianship report.

Table 5.4
Information gathered about the carer

Information gathered about carers	Carers				Social worker			
	Very much so %	To some degree %	No %	(n =)	Very much so %	To some degree %	No %	(n =)
Personal and family background and current relationships	78	16	6	50	88	12	0	59
Relationship to the child	82	14	4	49	93	7	0	59
Reasons for considering special guardianship	67	25	8	48	91	9	0	59
Family and household views on special guardianship	65	27	8	49	89	11	0	55
Health history	65	29	6	48	86	14	0	59
Education and employment history	47	40	13	48	81	19	0	58
Financial and housing circumstances	58	31	11	48	88	12	0	59
Experience of caring for children and attitude towards parenting	65	27	8	49	93	7	0	59
Feelings about child's contact with (other) birth family members	67	23	10	49	89	95	2	58
References – who will provide a personal reference for carer?	64	24	11	45	87	9	4	57

Table 5.5 shows good coverage of the child's personal, family background and relationships during assessment. Where this had not been addressed, the carers had been caring for the child for some time, either on a care order or residence order. It is possible, therefore, that much of the relevant information had been recorded by children's services in the past and that the current assessment was building on what was already known.

Coverage of some assessment areas appeared uneven, at least from the carers' perspective. In some areas, this was likely to reflect the age of the child concerned. Almost one-third of carers (and 13 per cent of social workers) reported that the child's wishes and feelings had not been considered. Although these cases all involved children below eight years of age, it is important that efforts are always made to ascertain what children want, even if they are very young or have lived with carers for a long time. Equally, some children were not yet of school age and coverage of educational history might not have been appropriate. With respect to exploring children's past placements, since some children had lived with relative carers from birth or the first few months of life, an exploration of this kind may not have been necessary. In cases where the child's culture, religious or language background had not been discussed (22%), all but two were described as White. It is therefore likely that the appropriateness of the placement had been assumed, although no social workers reported that it had not been considered.

Of course, the assessment process is a two-way exchange. In some cases, it provided carers with an opportunity to learn more about the child, their background and their needs. Several carers, particularly those who had not previously been through family court proceedings, commented that they had been unaware of the full extent of the child's past difficulties until the assessments began:

> *There was a file that big on my daughter and most of the things he was talking to me about I didn't know about and some I didn't even want to think about . . . Bearing in mind what's in the file, it was going to be a permanent thing.* (Grandmother)

Table 5.5
Information gathered about the child

Information gathered about child	Carers				Social worker			
	Very much so %	*To some degree* %	*No* %	*(n =)*	*Very much so* %	*To some degree* %	*No* %	*(n =)*
Child's personal and family background and relationships	74	18	**8**	49	90	10	**0**	59
Child's cultural, religious and language background	57	21	**22**	46	79	21	**0**	58
Details of existing court orders affecting the child	54	30	**16**	44	74	22	**4**	54
Places the child has lived	44	30	**26**	43	74	22	**3**	58
Child's own wishes and feelings about special guardianship	49	19	**32**	41	64	23	**13**	53
Child's health history	58	20	**22**	45	84	16	**0**	58
Child's education history	46	27	**27**	41	75	19	**6**	53
Child's physical, emotional and behavioural needs	57	28	**15**	47	90	10	**0**	59
Child's contact with (other) birth relatives	61	30	**9**	46	86	14	**0**	59
Child's interests, likes and dislikes	51	26	**23**	43	82	16	**2**	55

The assessment experience

The interviews with carers revealed mixed experiences of the assessment process. For some, the process had been relatively straightforward, especially where previous assessments had already been undertaken.

It wasn't too onerous. It was like building a profile and a lot of that they pulled from the foster care assessment. (Unrelated foster carer)

Overall, most carers noted that once things got going the process of gaining the order was fairly smooth. However, this does glide over some of the jolts that occurred along the way. For a number of carers, the assessment process had seemed overly intrusive and intense. Some described a stream of different professionals coming to talk with them and taking personal details:

The number of people involved was just too many, two social workers, the Children's Guardian, their solicitors, the mum's solicitors. (Aunt)

In my experience, there were too many professionals involved. I had one assessment, but had to do it all again as that social worker moved on and the new one wanted to re-assess, so it just went on and on. (Grandmother)

Others commented on the depth of detail required, their sense of being under surveillance or suspicion and the protracted period of time over which assessment took place, especially when social workers changed, paperwork was lost and assessments repeated. In these circumstances, the process was viewed as intense and draining:

It was very personal. They asked my life history, who I was married to, when I was married, what sort of background I came from, what my ex-husband was like, did he beat me up? They talked to friends and to family, what did they think? (Grandmother)

They lost the paperwork. What they had done they had to come back and do again, and staff, I've never seen as many staff, because each time we had a meeting there was somebody else. That person had changed or gone off sick. (Grandmother)

Where unrelated or kinship carers had previously been assessed under fostering regulations or for residence orders, there was often a feeling of re-telling the same stories, of information being unnecessarily duplicated:

One minute it was kinship assessment, then a psychological assessment, then the [special] guardian assessment. They kept asking me the same questions. (Grandmother)

Those who had undergone multiple or consecutive assessments had frequently become confused about precisely what they were being assessed for, when and at what stage in the process they were.

It is understandable that some carers, particularly those who had been caring for their child for some years prior to application, would feel that the assessment process was unnecessarily intrusive or protracted:

It's very difficult for somebody who's had the child for so many years. You think, he's a member of the family, why do you need this? (Grandmother)

These experiences led some carers to query whether a more condensed version of assessment might be possible where the child had been living with them for several years or where carers had been subject to other lengthy assessments in the recent past.

Despite these variable and occasionally unsatisfactory experiences, most carers acknowledged the importance of thorough assessment for safeguarding children:

They check and double check and re-check. Obviously it's for the welfare and the safety of the child and there's nothing more precious than a child, so it's done for a reason and I thinks it's all valid, every bit. (Grandmother)

These are challenging issues for practitioners. Recent studies on family and friends care have highlighted the importance of assessment, showing some association with the quality and durability of placements, although what makes for good assessment in kinship settings is still less certain (see Farmer and Moyers, 2008; Hunt *et al*, 2008). Our findings suggest that a good balance needs to be struck between the safeguarding of children and the development of assessment formats that are flexible, inclusive and not too off-putting to families and long-term carers. Thoroughness, however, is a critical issue. The profile of carers and children currently seeking special guardianship means that local authorities are making long-term permanence decisions, often involving very young children. The assessment question, therefore, is not just whether carers will be good enough parents now, but also whether they will be good enough parents until the child reaches adulthood. As the policy interviews showed (see Chapter 3), the timescales for completing assessments in special guardianship cases are tight, much tighter than is the case in adoption assessments. There was also evidence that, due to these restrictions, some compromises had to be made, both with respect to coverage and quality assurance procedures (see also Hall, 2008).

In these circumstances, the risks to children can be increased, as can the risk of later breakdown at a stage when other permanence options may have been reduced by age. Assessment is not just about testing the suitability of carers. It is also about helping them to prepare for the task ahead. If carers are not properly prepared for the challenges that may lie ahead, through individual counselling or preparatory support groups, then, perhaps especially if they have not yet lived with the child, these risks can be magnified. Balancing these different aspects of the assessment process takes time. Yet in special guardianship cases, time appears to be of the essence.

Almost all carers (97%), however, had been supported by children's services in their special guardianship application. Furthermore, in one-third of cases (32%), the decision to support the application had been made in consultation with members of a permanence panel and in two-fifths (41%), a senior social work manager had supported the application. Only two applicants, for whom we have information, had not been supported by children's services. These were opposed due to concerns about the carers' ability to protect the children from potentially harmful or disruptive contact with the birth parents. In both cases, a special guardianship order was granted by the court.

Court hearing and outcome

Approximately two-thirds of cases (63%) had reached a court decision within the study timeframe. Timescales from application to decision were available for only around one-quarter of cases, due to limited data on the dates of application and the dates of the court decision supplied by carers and social workers. These timescales ranged from one month, in a case where the court had granted an order during the course of other proceedings, to 15 months, where documentation had been lost or court hearings had been subject to delays.

A small number of carers felt that the process had been 'rushed through'. One foster carer noted that she felt the local authority was keen to speed things up even though the children had lived with her for less than a year at the time of application. Although she felt things had worked out well on this occasion, she commented on the risks of embarking upon a long-term commitment too early in the care relationship:

> *The children seemed to be only with us a year and then it was suddenly push, push ... We were pressured and I think you really need to get to know the children first. Sometimes a year is not long enough and the children were taken and asked questions and they'd say to me, 'We were asked questions but we didn't understand because we haven't been with you long enough to find out.' I'm glad I did it, but I wish I had longer to get to know them and for them to get to know me and [my husband].* (Unrelated foster carer, caring for a sibling group of four)

It is certainly a concern that special guardianship might be fast tracked, especially in cases where the carer and child have a relatively new relationship or have not previously lived together. The legislation does not stipulate a minimum period of residency. As we have seen, it was not unusual for children to have been living elsewhere prior to the order being granted. This was the case for around one-quarter (24%) of those in the current study. While this had generally involved a move to a known family member, one might expect nonetheless that some period of adjustment would be necessary to test the new situation, and yet this is likely to occur only after a decision has been made to award permanency and when there is little opportunity for services to intercede. As one social worker noted:

I think it is an excellent order for families. However, it sometimes appears that it is granted too easily to those who may not be as easily prepared.

In contrast, some carers were surprised or dismayed at the delays involved in reaching a court decision. This was sometimes the result of a protracted assessment process, inadequate court reports or the postponement of court hearings:

We went to court about six times because of [the case] being chucked out because the support package wasn't enough and there was a lack of information that the judge needed. He couldn't understand the reports. (Adult cousin)

Aside from the inconvenience caused by cancelled court hearings, it also generated increased anxiety or disappointment for carers and children who had geared themselves up for their day in court:

We stopped telling [her] when the court dates were because it just seemed like we were building everything up and then, literally a few days before, it got cancelled. (Unrelated foster carer)

Apprehension about the court process was certainly evident amongst carers. Several talked of feeling stressed or nervous and described the experience as 'daunting', 'scary' or 'nerve-wracking'. It seemed, however, that some had been better prepared for the experience than others. Around one-half (51%) of carers said they had received advice about what to expect from the court process:

Our solicitor, the guardian and the social worker, they gave us some idea of what it was going to be like, how big it is and who's going to be involved with the judge. (Aunt)

The social workers kept saying: 'It's nothing to worry about; it'll be a really nice day.' (Unrelated foster carer)

However, the other half (49%) reported receiving no advice or support to help them prepare for court and two-fifths (40%) had apparently not been advised about the decisions the court could make: 'It was a bit of an unknown, really' (Grandmother).

Among the more positive experiences, were examples where carers had felt well supported throughout the process and were confident that there was a common goal: 'We were all singing from the same hymn sheet.' One carer explained how she had been made to feel at ease in court, although this probably had as much to do with the lack of controversy surrounding this case as anything else:

We just sat round a table and talked. The judge was really nice and I didn't feel frightened and the judge said, 'I'll grant [the order] for you', and that was it. Nobody contested it at all. I think that's what made it better; we were all – my solicitor, their solicitor, the social worker – all on the same side. (Grandmother)

Court decisions

Of the 75 cases that had reached a court decision, all had been granted a special guardianship order. Most of these cases involved kinship carers (67%), while a third (33%) involved unrelated foster carers. Only one carer reported that she had not been happy with the decision. She noted that her preference remained adoption, but she felt she had no choice but to accept the court's decision.

In granting the order, the court may decide to make an additional order. In a majority of cases, no other orders were made. In at least two cases, the court made provision for a change of surname for the child. Both cases had the permission of birth parents to do so.

In one-third of cases (33%), the court also sanctioned the making or changing of contact orders for birth parents and other relatives. In the majority of cases, therefore, the onset of special guardianship had not greatly disturbed the patterns of family contact that had preceded it. Contact orders were made in favour of birth mothers in just over one-quarter of cases (26%) and of birth fathers in around one-fifth (21%). Just one father had an order preventing further contact with his child. In relation to other family members, contact orders were made in favour of siblings (six per cent) and other relatives (12%) in just a small proportion of cases, probably because they were not considered necessary to guarantee that contact would continue.

For almost one in ten special guardianship orders made (nine per cent), however, the court had attached a supervision order. This amounted to seven cases, four of which were kinship carers and three were unrelated foster carers. There was some indication that this was more common in certain jurisdictions, as just over half were located in one local authority.

The reasons for attaching a supervision order reflected concerns about the level of support that might be required by some carers. In at least three cases, the supervision order was intended to guarantee access to local authority resources during the first year. In one case, this was to enable the local authority to resource and supervise contact with the child's birth family. In two cases, however, the supervision order was put in place to offer greater protection to the child during the early months by providing children's services with some leverage to monitor progress. In these cases, it would appear that concerns around the special guardian's ability to cope with current or anticipated difficulties were evident at the time of the court decision. It also begs the question whether (at least at that time) a special guardianship order had been the right one for the child.

The use of supervision orders was also apparent in Hall's (2008) study, where a higher proportion of supervision orders had been attached (24%). Hall raised a number of questions in relation to this practice, which find resonance with our own findings. First, given that the special guardian-ship regulations require local authorities to make provision for post-order support, it is surprising that court officials should feel the need to fall back on supervision orders to guarantee access to these resources. Second, it implies a lack of confidence in the ability of some special guardians to protect and care for the child and, third, it echoes concerns highlighted earlier in this chapter about the limited powers available to children's services to monitor or intervene should difficulties arise once a special guardianship order has been granted.

Becoming a special guardian

Any fears or dissatisfaction about the lead up to the court decision appeared not to have dampened the positive feelings expressed once the order had been granted. As one carer who had experienced the highs and lows, expressed it, 'We jumped for joy and sang "I belong to you and you belong to me".'

While some carers felt that the decision meant little more than the "official stamp" on an existing and quite long-standing relationship, many others felt it represented an important and emotional step forward in their own lives and those of their children:

We were over the moon, very happy, because now [she] can settle down and be part of the family. (Step-grandfather)

We were relieved and happy to [be] starting a fresh chapter of a normal life. (Unrelated foster carer)

I cried when I came out and my solicitors said: 'What are you crying for, you got it?' But it's a big thing. (Grandmother)

Although some of the children in this study were too young to understand or comment on the implications of their new legal status, carers described the impact the court's decision had on their children: 'The children were excited.'

She felt very happy that her mum could no longer take her away, and that she didn't have to live with her. (Grandmother)

Finally, for one carer, 15 months of assessments and court cases had been concluded with her becoming special guardian of her young niece, 'and that was the best day when we walked out of court'.

Achieving special guardianship had often been the end of a long and difficult journey. In the next chapter, we pick up the story to see how things were turning out for those who had achieved it and for those who were still making their way along the road.

Summary

- Slightly more carers (53%) had chosen to apply for special guardianship than had been advised to apply for or accept a special guardianship order (47%). In 11 per cent of cases, the order had been made in the course of other private or public law proceedings.
- A range of professionals had assisted carers in the decision to apply, including social workers, solicitors and children's guardians, reflecting the high proportion of children in or on the edge of the care system and those who were already involved in court proceedings.
- There was some evidence of a lack of knowledge amongst social work and legal services. Some carers had encountered uncertainty about what special guardianship involved, how to apply for it, how it compared to other permanence options and what it would mean for them in practice. This was largely attributed to the "early days" of the new order, as many applicants were amongst the first in their local authority. Nevertheless, it suggests the need to raise awareness through detailed practice guidance and comprehensive training for relevant professionals.
- Carers identified a range of motivating factors that influenced their decision to apply. The desire to provide a secure and loving home for the child within the family and outside of the care system was a key incentive. Special guardianship was also considered a more secure and robust option than residence orders and was often perceived as preferable to adoption, particularly for kinship carers who wished to avoid complicating family relationships or having their child adopted out of the family.
- Though most local authorities had based their assessment procedures on the official regulations and guidance, there was considerable concern amongst practitioners about the short timescales for completing assessments and difficulties involved in quality assuring the work that was done. One-third of cases were scrutinised by a

permanence panel and two-fifths by a senior manager.

- Carers, however, often felt that the assessment process could be protracted and "intrusive". Though carers generally acknowledged the need for thoroughness, they were frustrated when information was duplicated and by delays, cancelled court dates and the number of different professionals asking "personal" questions. These concerns are likely to reflect the number of carers who had been caring for the child for several years prior to the assessment and those who had already been assessed as foster carers. It is important, therefore, that assessments build on and do not simply duplicate those previously undertaken.

- Overall, responses from carers and social workers suggested that most core areas had been covered during the assessment. There was some evidence that one or two carers had been awarded an order during the course of other court proceedings, without a special guardianship assessment and report having been completed.

- Almost two-thirds of the cases (63%) had reached a court decision. All had been granted a special guardianship order. In one-third of cases (33%), the court had sanctioned the making or changing of contact orders and in nine per cent of cases a supervision order had been attached. These were made to secure access to local authority services or to provide the local authority with some leverage where there were concerns about how some carers might cope.

- The response to the court decision was overwhelmingly positive. Carers commented on how special guardianship marked a new start for themselves and the child and offered the chance of legal and emotional security for their family.

- Issues emerging from the assessment and court process carry implications for services, including the need for clear guidance and information, greater awareness amongst relevant professionals and clarity for carers around timescales and procedures for the assessment and what they can expect in terms of support. Finally, services face the challenge of ensuring that the assessment process is comprehensive and robust so that safe decisions can be made, but also that they are not unduly off-putting to those carers who have already been assessed or have had long-term care of the child.

6 Placement experiences, well-being and birth family relationships

This chapter explores how the children and their carers were getting on together, identifies issues that have arisen in these and wider family relationships and considers the impact of special guardianship on the parenting role of guardians. It also describes the progress and well-being of these children in relation to home, school, personal development and behaviour. In doing so, we draw on the survey data collected from carers and social workers and on the interviews conducted with carers and children.

At the time of data collection, 77 carers had 113 children living with them.[41] In total, 60 of these carers had already obtained special guardianship orders and a further 16 were still in the process of applying.[42]

The sections below on placement experience and progress, on child well-being and birth family relationships include findings on all 113 children, even though some of these were not yet special guardianship families. However, the mainly qualitative sections that provide a focus on the impact of special guardianship on parenting, perceptions of permanence and on contact orders include only those cases where a special guardianship order was known to have been obtained.

The rationale for this rests on the hypothesis that the earlier sections are unlikely to be affected greatly by the granting of a special guardianship order. They tend to be much more about the experience of living together and the quality of placement and family relationships. There would be a problem if those still seeking an order had been living together for much less time than those who had been granted one. The reverse, however, tended to be the case. A larger proportion of those still awaiting

---

[41] Six children had not yet moved in with their carers. All were still living in unrelated foster placements and have therefore been excluded from all analyses in this chapter. In addition, a further case has been excluded as the application for special guardianship had been withdrawn.

[42] The outcome of the application was missing in one additional case.

an order (62%) had been living with their carer for three or more years than was the case for those already subject to an order (24%).[43]

Only one in seven (14%) had been living with their carers for less than one year, a comparable proportion to those with an order (13%). There was also no significant difference in the age distribution of these two groups of children at data collection (p 0.44).

Placement progress and relationships

The majority of the children were living with relative carers. Amongst those living with carers at data collection (n = 113), just over one-half (51%) had already been living with relatives on care or residence orders before the special guardianship application was made. A further 14 per cent had been living with relatives on an informal basis. These placements then continued. One-third of the children (33.5%) had been placed in non-relative foster care prior to a special guardianship order being made, with 20 per cent moving to relatives and just 13.5 per cent staying on with these non-relative carers through special guardianship.[44] As indicated above, the majority had been in their current placement for some time at data collection.

Taken overall, the assessment of these placements by carers and social workers was encouraging. The majority of carers (76%) and social workers (83%) reported that things had gone 'very well'. One in five carers (20%), however, felt that the placement had gone 'as well as could be expected' and for four per cent, 'not very well'. These ratings appear higher than those found in recent studies of kinship care more generally and may reflect a tendency for special guardianship to be taken up by families where circumstances appear propitious and relationships more firmly cemented (Farmer and Moyers, 2008; Hunt et al, 2008).[45] There

---

[43]   Mann-Whitney U exact test: p<0.01; n = 96.

[44]   Two children had been living with birth parent(s) before moving to live with relatives.

[45]   Comparisons are also inexact, since these studies assessed placement quality through researcher ratings derived from analysis of social work case files. However, Hunt and colleagues found that 36 per cent of placements were problem free, 44 per cent had some problems and 20 per cent had major concerns. Farmer and Moyers found that 66 per cent of kin placements were 'satisfactory'.

was no difference in these assessments for kin or unrelated foster care placements or according to the length of time children had lived with their carers (p = 0.58).

Since two-thirds of the children had lived with these carers for two or more years, these were unlikely to have been "honeymoon period" ratings. However, we do need to bear in mind that many of these children were young (7% aged nine or under). Research on foster care has shown that disruption rates are significantly higher for adolescents than for younger children (Sinclair *et al*, 2005b, 2005c). It is therefore likely that difficulties in some of these placements may arise in the future. This will be more likely where children display challenging behaviour, since emotional and behavioural difficulties at the start of placement (at any age) are associated with higher placement disruption rates (Sinclair, 2005). Where carers and social workers felt that the placements had only gone 'as well as could be expected', two factors proved significant in this dataset: it was more likely to have been the case for boys rather than girls and for children considered to have greater emotional and behavioural difficulties.[46]

Social workers were very much of the opinion that these placements were "very" (81%) or "quite" (16%) suitable for the needs of these children. The benefits that social workers perceived were those that may accrue from long-term placements. The children were considered to have settled well and made good progress, to have developed close attachments to their carers and, in the main, to be happy, secure and thriving. Where placed with relatives, comments also focused on the perceived benefits of long-term relationships with their carers, integration within the wider family and, especially for children from minority ethnic backgrounds, of positive cultural connections.

Kinship

Children are with family and have an established and settled relationship with them.

---

[46] The placement was reported to have gone '*very well*' for 96 per cent of girls as compared to 78 per cent of boys (Fisher's Exact Test: p<0.01; n = 110); emotional and behavioural difficulties significant at p<0.01 (Mann-Whitney U Exact Test, n = 102).

The child has a positive attachment with his grandmother and feels safe and secure in this environment. Aunt is a very able carer. Child will have an opportunity to be brought up in his family and will have ongoing contact with his mother and other relatives.

Unrelated foster care
Placed with siblings. First placement; settled very well. Carer willing to offer permanence within a few weeks of placing.

Child happy and thriving in placement and maintains a distant family link.

Even where placements were considered "suitable", some social workers expressed lingering concerns about the challenges some carers had taken on, about the appropriateness of some parenting styles and about the ability of carers to protect children where contact arrangements were difficult. In a case involving two siblings, two separate child protection referrals had been made and the carer had applied to discharge the special guardianship order, suggesting that a breakdown in the placement was imminent.

Despite these worries, in most cases social workers had few concerns about the safety of children in their current placement. Almost three-quarters (74%) reported no concerns and a further fifth 'very few' concerns (21%). Apart from the child protection cases above – and another where there was some evidence of a child being left in the care of unsafe adults – most concerns centred on potential future risks. These included threats by birth parents to remove children (not yet acted on), worries about how carers would manage future challenging behaviours linked to past maltreatment, and about contact with violent or substance-misusing family members. In one instance, concern was linked to the absence of adequate adaptations for a disabled child in the home, although there was no evidence that this had been acted upon by children's services.

The interviews with carers and children revealed the close relationships that had grown over time. Grandparent carers, who were in the majority, had often had a share in the child's care from birth and the close bonds that had been established with their grandchildren were often evident, together with the insecurities of children stemming from past maltreatment or disruption:

We're very close. We have our moments . . . but we always have a kiss and cuddle and make up. He's very insecure . . . because so many people have left him in his life . . . it's made him very insecure. So . . . if he goes to his bedroom, [within] five minutes he'll have to come in to make sure I'm still here . . . just to tell me he loves me and then he'll go back to his bedroom. (Grandparent)

Where relationships with relatives or former foster carers were longstanding, children had tended to be absorbed into the everyday rhythms of wider family life, their presence almost taken for granted:

He's been around . . . from when he was little . . . So he's just been part of the family all his life. (Unrelated former foster carer)

Relationships with birth or substitute siblings, grandparents, aunts, uncles or cousins appeared to be largely woven into the everyday world of the children. While we were only able to interview three children, all of whom were living with unrelated former foster carers, they also expressed a sense of being loved, secure and part of the family – although this was often stated in more prosaic terms:

'Cos they're always with us. 'Cos we can talk to them when we've got any problems that we need to talk about . . . It makes me feel part of this family 'cos mum lets us join in with all the fun they're doing. They don't let us miss out on anything, but we're always there when they're having fun.

As children felt more secure in these relationships, some were able to open up more about the distress they had experienced in the past. Others kept this burden more private and were more distant. In these circumstances, carers sometimes struggled to gauge the extent to which this distance was part of the normal spectrum of childhood behaviour:

As he's getting older . . . I think he's getting a little bit distant . . . I suppose sometimes you read a bit too much into [his] past and maybe make some excuses as to the reasons why he is the way he is. Maybe he would just have been like that anyway.

An argument presented against adoption in family settings is that it tends to distort the structure of family relationships and it is a factor (among many others) that the court takes into account when weighing evidence in individual cases (Bainham, 2007; Bond, 2007). While special guardianship certainly does not imply a final legal severance with birth parents, these issues are nonetheless live in special guardianship families. Placement with relatives tended to involve just such a reordering of family relationships. This was confusing for some younger children and potentially difficult questions were inevitably asked. Some carers discussed these questions in interview and felt that an honest and open approach was the best way to reduce this confusion, as suggested by one adult cousin looking after a two-year-old girl:

She calls me mamma, which I have tried to put her straight about, because she then goes and calls her [birth mother] mamma . . . I don't mind, but when she says it I try to let her know what mamma is, what cousin is, so she doesn't get confused.

Similar explanations were also required for children in the wider family or for friends at school. One grandparent, for example, reported fielding questions from all her other grandchildren about her relationship with the grandson living with her and why he was not living with his birth mother:

They've all asked that question . . . well, not so much the little ones but as they get older . . . [We] haven't gone into full details, you know, but to them it has just become a way of life.

Where children had been living with carers for a long time, this restructuring of relationships could be handled in a fairly natural way. In these circumstances, the transition to special guardianship (from the legal relationship that preceded it) did not greatly affect the pattern of everyday relationships; life continued much as it had before. This is not to say that these placements were untroubled or that children did not present significant challenges to their carers. However, the quality of relationships that had been established did demonstrate the high degree of commitment to the placement shown by carers and the children in their care. This was reflected by the responses of the social workers involved in these cases.

When asked to assess the degree to which different parties were committed to the placement, social workers reported a very high degree of commitment by carers (96%), children (89%) and other children in the household (90%) not placed under special guardianship. Recent research has pointed to a difference in the level of commitment shown by kinship carers and unrelated foster carers, with the former being more likely to show very high levels of commitment (Farmer and Moyers, 2008). This difference was not evident in a special guardianship context, although we must be mindful of the small number of cases involved in this analysis. Perhaps, not surprisingly, birth parents were considered more ambivalent, with only 44 per cent being "fully" committed, 47 per cent having "some" commitment and nine per cent "none". The implications of this greater ambivalence for relationships between carers, children and birth parents is considered further below.

Child well-being

This section draws on survey data gathered from carers and social workers in relation to all children living with their carers to consider their progress and well-being in some key developmental areas – health, education, emotional ties, friendships, skills, confidence and behaviour. Respondents were asked to rate their child in relation to a number of well-being indicators according to how they had been faring over the previous three months. In order to maximise the information on children and reduce the amount of missing data, we have merged the responses provided by social workers and carers. Where carers provided a return, we took their view since they were likely to know the children best. Where we only had one return for a child (from social worker or carer), we included that.[47] These findings are presented in Table 6.1.

---

[47] For children living with their carers (n = 113), we received 44 questionnaires from carers and social workers, 40 from just social workers and 29 from carers only.

Table 6.1
Child well-being indicators

	Poor %	Quite poor %	Quite good %	Good %	Number (n)
Health (frequently ill and/or failing to thrive, normally well and thriving)	1	3	8	88	n = 109
Educational progress (relative to age and ability)	3	10	43	44	n = 99
Skills and interests	2	13	48	38	n = 96
Self-confidence	3	10	43	44	n = 100
Emotional ties (to at least one adult)	1	4	21	74	n = 105
Close friends	2	11	44	43	n = 98
Emotional and behavioural difficulties	5	13	48	34	n = 102
Self-care skills (competence for age)	0	7	34	59	n = 101
Emotional well-being (sad, unhappy; normally happy)	0	6	31	63	n = 106

By all accounts, these children were perceived to be faring quite well at the point of data collection, perhaps especially in relation to their health, attachments and emotional well-being. In order to see whether the overall well-being of these children was associated with other factors, these variables were combined to provide an overall well-being score for each child. Reliability analysis suggested there was a good degree of internal consistency between these measures (Cronbach's Alpha 0.862): that each item was measuring a similar kind of thing. The combined measure provided a score for each child within the range 9–34, with higher scores being more positive.

Research on fostering and kinship care suggests that where children are placed at an older age the chances of subsequent breakdown are significantly increased (Sinclair, 2005; Farmer and Moyers, 2008; Hunt *et al*, 2008). Hunt and colleagues found that age at the conclusion of care proceedings was also associated with later well-being and overall placement outcome. Although our data are not directly comparable, since it is based on age at data collection, there was also some (albeit weak) association between age and overall well-being. Older children tended to be faring less well than those who were younger.[48] There was also some evidence that boys were faring rather less well than girls; although this did not reach the threshold for significance ($p = 0.07$), but this association did hold for children with learning disabilities in relation to education, social skills and behaviour.[49]

Although there was no association between how children were faring and ethnic origin, placement with siblings, past history of abuse or neglect, or continuing social work contact, there was some association with type of placement. The well-being of children was perceived to be lower for those living with unrelated former foster carers in relation to life and social skills, friendships and behaviour than was the case for those living with relatives.[50]

Although, overall, the children appeared to be faring quite well, they were clearly not untroubled children. At least two-thirds had previously

---

[48] Kendall's tau-b Test: $p = 0.05$; *tau* –0.154; $n = 88$.

[49] Mann-Whitney U Exact Test: $p = 0.03$; $n = 88$.

[50] Mann Whitney U Exact Test: $p = 0.03$; $n = 85$.

been looked after by local authorities. Many came from families troubled by mental health problems, substance misuse or domestic violence, and around two-thirds had been placed as a result of risks to their safety or a failure to thrive. Around one-quarter had emotional, behavioural or learning problems. In these circumstances, the degree to which they were perceived to be settled and doing well is encouraging. However, some of the parenting challenges that can arise were also revealed through the interviews with special guardians.

Some children were described by carers as being relatively easy to care for – 'as easy as kids go'. More often these comments were associated with babies or very young children, as suggested by a grandmother caring for a child aged 18 months:

> *[She's an] angel by nature. She's been a bit clingy since we came back off holiday, but most of the time she eats well, she sleeps well. She's just a perfect little baby.*

Although most children were considered normally healthy, some carers worried about the physical and emotional health needs of their children. Some children had chronic health problems that required careful management, including eczema, asthma and other acute respiratory problems that had required frequent periods of hospitalisation. Some children had experienced or even witnessed the untimely deaths of birth parents or older siblings through misuse of drugs or alcohol or through suicide linked to acute mental health problems. In one instance, a former foster carer described the frustration experienced by a child with a serious long-term blood disorder and, by implication, the close daily monitoring that was required of her:

> *It doesn't really affect him at the moment because he doesn't understand. He keeps saying, 'Why do I have to have all these special injections? Why do I have to keep going to the hospital and seeing these special doctors?' What hurts [him] the most is that he loves sport and he can't do it.*

Worries about the future were also evident. Where children had experienced serious abuse or neglect or where families had a history of mental health problems, carers often expressed worry about the psychological consequences for children as they grew up, how they would manage these and whether support would still be available at that stage.

These past experiences also brought problems in the present, manifested through a range of attachment and behaviour difficulties. Some carers described their children as being sad and tearful at times and this could be heightened for a time after contact with key birth relatives. Some described children as being withdrawn or overly clingy and attention seeking. The insecurities underlying these behaviours often made it difficult for carers to obtain any respite or space for themselves:

We are close. He's my shadow. Because of things that have happened to him, he gets very upset. I can't be anywhere without [him]. [He] is lost, you know . . . Respite wasn't good for him. Three people had . . . said they don't want him because . . . he shows such bad behaviour they can't control it. Now [they were families]. I'm on my own with him. (Unrelated foster carer)

Difficulties manifested through aggressive and defiant behaviour were not uncommon. This seemed to be especially the case where children had been neglected and had not experienced clear boundaries and routines. In these circumstances, efforts to impose controls could meet with considerable defiance:

He was . . . extremely aggressive . . . He would punch and scream; he would bite and head-butt . . . He was like a two-year-old in the body of a seven-year-old. [It was] as if he had lost a chunk of his childhood and he hadn't been taught anything . . . He had a really difficult time at home though. (Aunt)

[He] isn't a very easy little boy to care for. He's got such a lot of problems . . . He's a ten-year-old, but mentally he's not a ten-year-old . . . He's statemented at school, so he does have a lot of problems . . . There have been times when I've sat down and cried, he's got me so, you know, that I've just sat down and cried, and I think that possibly releases it, you know. [After] five minutes of crying I'm up . . . and we're alright . . . A lot of the times he's worth it. Because a

lot of the things he says and does, you think, now I know why I love him . . . It's not all bad, you know. (Grandmother)

The patience, understanding and commitment expressed in these comments frequently led carers to feel that progress had been made slowly, that their children had gradually calmed and, as they became more settled, the intensity of these behaviour difficulties had lessened over time. With this process of settlement, children were generally perceived to have acquired greater confidence in their verbal ability, physical appearance and gait:

She is very strong minded . . . [She] has really come out since she's lived here. She's more confident. She used to walk with her head down . . . She wasn't talking; she used to copy what you said . . . People say now that she walks tall and she's confident, her speech is confident, she's confident around everybody. (Grandmother, child four years old)

Research on looked after children and care leavers has consistently highlighted their poor educational progress and attainment (Social Exclusion Unit, 2003; Wade, 2006). However, some children who return to their families may fare worse educationally than those who remain in foster care (Sinclair *et al*, 2007); and evidence comparing children in kinship care with children in unrelated foster care is contradictory, with some studies suggesting the former may fare better and others that they tend to fare worse (Hunt, 2003).

School could also be a difficult arena for these children. As Table 6.1 suggested, children were less likely to have been perceived as making "good" progress in their education, in developing skills and interests, and in self-confidence than was the case in some other developmental areas. Most children were thought to have education deficits at the time of placement, although some had subsequently caught up with their classmates. Others continued to struggle and carers frequently mentioned children's problems with focus, concentration and confidence. For primary school children perceived as vulnerable, carers worried about how the transition to secondary school would be negotiated, especially where children had a relatively mild learning disability and would be attending large mainstream schools: '. . . with her education being so low, I'm just a bit concerned about her getting lost'. In these cases, carers were often attempting to liaise with special needs tutors to facilitate this transition and ensure schools were informed about issues of concern.

Some children, especially those statemented for their educational needs, had received additional support from teachers or educational psychologists. In some instances, the release of additional resources associated with the statementing process had brought gradual improvements:

> *He's doing a lot better since he's been statemented . . . I think he's always going to struggle . . . but the school are very helpful and I like to be kept in the loop . . . to know how he's doing, which they do . . . I can't really fault them at the minute.* (Grandmother)

The transition to special guardianship had also brought benefits. Children formerly looked after appreciated the normalisation of home-school relationships and the fact that social workers would no longer have direct involvement in school affairs:

> *I think for her it [special guardianship] was just a big relief. She was then going to be normal. She was not going to have that stigma attached to her, you know, with her [birth] parents having to go into school to have meetings with the head teacher and social worker . . . The only time we go into school now is when it's parents evening.* (Unrelated foster carer)

However, the transition could also bring new tensions. In at least two cases, frustrations grew when birth parents challenged the choice of school selected by guardian and child. In one instance, this was unsuccessfully pursued by a birth parent through solicitors and the courts.

The impact of special guardianship on carers and their families

Special guardianship is intended to give carers the right to exercise parental responsibility to the exclusion of others with an interest in the child, enabling them to make all of the key decisions affecting the daily lives of children in their care. Through this, it is intended to provide a permanent, legally secure placement at least until the child reaches the age of majority (Department for Education and Skills, 2005). One recent study found that special guardianship did appear to provide this for the majority of carers who had taken it up (Hall, 2008). This was also the case for the vast majority of carers responding to our survey who had special guardianship orders in place for a single child or a sibling group (n = 43). They felt the order did provide them with greater control over decisions affecting the child's life (97%) and greater legal security (97%). It was also perceived to reduce the possibility that children might be removed from them by birth parents or the local authority (91%), while at the same time enabling the child to retain a link with their birth parent(s) (74%). In these important respects, then, special guardianship was broadly meeting the expectations of carers.

Enhanced parental control was a prominent theme in interviews. In relation to children formerly looked after, the reduced role of children's services was broadly welcomed, as was freedom from the restrictions that generally apply to looked after children with respect to holidays abroad, school trips, medical treatment and sleepovers. Everyday family life had assumed a more normal quality. Special guardians also felt strengthened in negotiating contact arrangements with birth parents, even where relationships were quite difficult, or in taking important decisions affecting the child (for example, over choice of school or medical procedures) or in relation to more minor lifestyle choices that conflicted with birth parents' wishes. These negotiations were seldom easy and, in some cases, caused considerable stress and confusion amongst family members. Where the local authority was largely out of the picture, and its mediating or buffering function had gone, the implications of this greater parental responsibility (which had not always been freely chosen) were quite evident:

It's still better knowing the local authority's not involved . . . but it gives you greater responsibilities . . . It finally dawns on you that you are the one that's responsible for this child . . . You know there is no one you can call upon to say: 'Oh, this is happening, what should I do?' With special guardianship you have to . . . treat this child like she's yours now. So whatever decision you make, you have to make it with [her] in mind, what's best for her. So it does give you . . . control over everything. (Adult cousin)

There were alternative viewpoints. In particular, where children had been living in long-term kinship care the transition from being in "care" to special guardianship did not always bring discernible differences, perhaps especially where relationships with birth parents were also more harmonious:

I would say it wasn't any different to when he was on a care order . . . because I didn't have a lot of dealings with social services . . . and they weren't interfering in my life . . . It hasn't really made any difference . . . because [as well] dad's out of the picture . . . and mum's generally in agreement with everything. (Grandmother)

Special guardianship also provided greater legal security. There was a general sense of relief that the child finally belonged to their family and could be fully included in plans being made by the family in a natural way. It helped where there was general agreement that this was the right placement for the child and an acceptance of the parental role of guardians, as this reduced fears of future litigation. However, even where relations were more conflicted, there was often a sense of relief that the child or sibling group were no longer at risk of separation, care or adoption and could no longer be removed at the whim of a birth parent:

It puts your mind at rest, knowing that there's not going to be a knock at the door and it's going to be someone saying, 'She can have her kids back' . . . I've had him all these years, you're not having him back now. (Grandmother)

The transition to special guardianship had a considerable psychological and material impact on the lives of some carers and their families, a finding consistent with broader research on the impact of care-giving in kinship settings.[51] Even where young children had been considered relatively easy to care for, resuming a primary care role involved considerable sacrifice and adjustment to the life plans of carers. Some grandparent carers had to sacrifice plans for retirement. Some carers had to give up employment to meet the special needs of young children or to provide care to sibling groups, bringing household resources under greater strain. Most also sacrificed aspects (or all) of their own social lives. Alongside the reorienting of their own lives, kinship carers also had to manage their often contradictory feelings towards their sons and daughters, nephews and nieces through whom this situation had arisen and with whom contact arrangements generally continued. Although most found the caring role rewarding, it was often also exhausting:

> *Probably because I'm getting older, it's a lot, lot harder . . . This is it, 24/7. I can't even go out, that sounds bad doesn't it? . . . It's got to a point now that I've not been out in what, two years, and I just can't be bothered any more. I'd sooner just stay in, have a bath and go to bed.* (Grandmother, child two years old)

While carers did not generally regret the decision they had made, some had stepped forward primarily through a sense of familial obligation, and the strain of parenting young children once again was sometimes evident:

> *I'll be honest with you, it's wearing me down . . . It's had a big impact on me. I'm 47, when do I get a life? . . . I'm going to be 62 by the time she's 18 . . . I wish it hadn't happened.* (Grandmother, child three years old)

The settling-in period was particularly fraught. Additional stress was evident where employers refused to allow sufficient parental leave to allow carers to settle into their new role. In this respect, the distinction

---

[51] See Hunt (2003) for a helpful review of this literature.

made by employers between adoption and special guardianship leave entitlements was highlighted. Where homes were already crowded or a sibling group was being accommodated, some carers had to move home or make expensive adaptations to their existing one. Not all local authorities were prepared to assist them financially, thereby adding greatly to the financial strain on families.

Where other children were already living in the household, psychological adjustments had to be made. Even where the new child was well known and had stayed quite regularly in the past, some carers were taken aback by the initial strength of jealousies and rivalries between the children:

We didn't anticipate how my children's personalities would change having her here all the time. At first . . . they loved having her every Saturday and taking her back, but when she came all the time, after a couple of weeks [my children] were a bit put out. (Aunt)

Generally these difficulties calmed down over time, and, as relationships between children improved, some carers pointed to the benefits of children mixing and playing together:

It's easier when there's other children around because they entertain each other . . . They play together and it's less stressful . . . But when they go at each other . . . it's hard work. (Great-aunt, children five and six years old, and 11 months old)

Despite this range of difficulties, the survey findings showed that guardians were still convinced that special guardianship had been absolutely the right decision for the child (100%, n = 43) and, in the main, had been the right decision for them (81%) and their family (74%). The uncertainty reported at the margins for the carer and the carer's family reflects some of the real challenges in providing care that have been discussed above.[52]

---

[52] Only small numbers expressed this uncertainty. Twelve per cent (five) of carers felt "unsure" whether it had been the right decision for them or their family (three, 8%). Only one carer felt it had not.

Perceptions of permanence

The meaning of special guardianship was not clear to the three children we interviewed. They were confused about how it worked and whether or how it differed to adoption:

> *I think I've heard of that [special guardianship] . . . I think we talked about it before I went to court to get adopted . . . Oh, I can't remember what it means really.* (Girl, nine years old)

The explanations provided to children by carers were couched in terms appropriate to their age and understanding, as was the case with this child:

> *All [she] knew was that . . . she was going to stay with us forever . . . The first thing she asked was, 'Can I call you mum and dad now?' Because she'd been asking and we'd kept saying 'no' . . . So we've never really gone into the ins and outs about the difference between adoption and special guardianship because . . . I don't know if she needs to know.* (Unrelated foster carer)

Finding ways of explaining the reasons that underlay their separation from birth parents was not easy, although most carers opted for a careful but relatively direct approach:

> *The way I explained it to him is that his mum has got an illness which is not a physical illness, it's to do with the way her mind works . . . and people have decided that she might not be able to do the best thing for him, so they decided that he would live here.* (Aunt, boy 10 years old)

Maintaining a record of events in children's lives was also important for some carers, creating a life story that would be available to children as they grew up:

> *I keep a [record] of everything he does . . . I have all the paperwork from the court cases and I will keep it for him so that he has . . . some understanding of how it all evolved . . . He can then make [his own] decisions when he's an adult.* (Great aunt, boy six years old)

What appeared to matter more to children was not the particular legal arrangement that bound them to their carers but the feeling of psychological permanence that accrued from carers making a long-term commitment to them (see Gleeson *et al*, 1997; Altshuler, 1999). Children's sense of permanence and belonging grew through feelings of safety, security and gradual inclusion within the wider family network, irrespective of whether they were placed with foster carers or relatives. Where children had experienced a considerable amount of past movement and disruption, what mattered most was feeling they may have a settled future:

> *I think my [new] mum wanted me to stay 'cos she'd seen me before . . . and she thought I was going to be a really nice child for her . . . Before I came here I was with my tummy mummy and then I moved 'cos she wasn't looking after me properly, and then I kept moving and moving and moving . . . [It] made me feel that I didn't live [anywhere] . . . It's much, much better here.* (Girl, nine years old, ex-foster care)

Similar views about the need for children to settle within a permanent home were expressed by carers:

> *By the time the legal guardianship was sorted, she'd had two social workers and two foster carers. So she'd [had] that situation with her mum and [then was] shifted from place to place. I felt that it was time she settled down.* (Grandmother, girl six years old)

Names were also significant for a developing sense of belonging. This is also more complex (and sometimes fraught) territory in special guardianship when compared to adoption. In two cases, a surname change had been granted by the court at the time of the special guardianship application. In some others, children had themselves made an informal decision to hyphenate their surnames, to signify their presence in both families, and one or two carers living with partners suggested that children might apply for a name change in the future should the partners decide to marry. In a sense, this mirrors children's preoccupation with the name by which they could know their carers. Some foster carers and relatives, worried about the confusion that might be caused to children, started out by trying to maintain a clear distinction between their status and that of the birth parents. However, over time, most seemed to have relented and allowed children to call them "Mum" or "Dad" (or a variance thereof), recognising that it helped children to find a better "fit" within the family unit:

> *I thought it would be too confusing, him having two mums . . . a mum that he lived with and a mum that he saw four times a year . . . I thought, well I'm not his mum . . . Maybe I wasn't looking at it from his point of view . . . He knows he has a mum . . . he knows her by name and he knows that's his mum . . . So sometimes he calls me that . . . and when people refer to them as brothers he accepts that . . . So I think he's beginning to realise what fits and what doesn't, what feels more comfortable for him and what he likes.* (Great-aunt)

Helping children to construct feelings of belonging and permanence took considerable time and care. It was made more difficult where tensions were evident in relationships with birth parents. In these circumstances, contact with a birth parent could mean children receiving negative or mixed messages about whose children they really were, how long they might stay and whether they would return. Inevitably, this resulted in confusion for children and anxiety for their primary carers. Not only would they have to deal with the day-to-day behavioural consequences or questions that were raised, but also it created anxiety about whether their right to care would be challenged in the future:

> *We're trying to build a family unit. We're trying to say you are part of our family unit, you are our child, we love you the same as the rest. She's going to see her [birth mother] and she's telling her it's all a lie . . . which is taking away the security we're trying to give her.* (Aunt, child three years old)

Although developing case law suggests that courts take into account the quality of these relationships when deciding between special guardianship and adoption, it is in such circumstances that the permanency limitations of special guardianship are most obviously exposed. Two interviewees had wanted to proceed to adoption, precisely because of these concerns, but had been persuaded by local authorities and/or the court to accept a special guardianship outcome. Some carers also reported that if birth parents ever pressed for an increased level of contact they would consider seeking adoption, suggesting that these relationships were also not without difficulty.[53] Where carers had anxieties about the potential for future legal challenge, the newness of special guardianship meant they were sometimes unaware of what precisely needed to change for such a challenge to be successful. In these scenarios, the additional security afforded through adoption was attractive, as suggested by the aunt quoted above:

We don't know what the actual grey area is of them challenging to take her back . . . We really don't know what grounds it would be . . . God forbid, but if we were to get divorced would that be sufficient grounds? We don't know . . . The [special] guardianship shouldn't have been considered because it's given her false hope that she can fight for her back one day.

Fortunately, the survey findings suggest that cases of this kind may be in the minority. Most special guardians felt confident that they would be able to provide a "permanent home" for their child and a "family for life" (80% and 81% respectively). Most, as we have seen, also thought special guardianship had been the right order for them. However, the fact that around one-fifth of guardians had significant permanence doubts is a matter for concern. In some cases, events within the placement were not going well and, in one or two instances, were approaching breakdown. In others, perceptions of permanence were affected by ongoing relationships within the wider family.

---

[53] Although a special guardianship order cannot be challenged without leave of the court and applicants must show a "significant change" in circumstances, there is no restriction on applications for s.8 orders for contact, prohibited steps or specific issues, unless these rights have been limited by the court under s.91(14) of the Children Act 1989 (Masson *et al*, 2008a).

Birth family contact and relationships

For children living in stranger care or kinship settings, contact with birth parents is complicated terrain.[54] A perceived advantage of special guardianship lies in the preservation of family links and relationships. For looked after children and young people leaving care, the benefits of maintaining continuity in family relationships, where it is feasible and safe to do so, have been a consistent theme in the literature (Millham *et al*, 1986; Biehal *et al*, 1995; Berridge, 1997). Levels of family contact are now higher amongst looked after children and "drift" away from families is less common. However, a cautionary note about the implications of negative contact for child and placement has also been written; contact with some family members is not an unequivocal good (Quinton *et al*, 1997; Sinclair *et al*, 2005c). In addition, as our policy data has suggested (see Chapter 3), worries about the loss of local authority mediation and support and the self-management of birth family relationships appears to have acted as an important deterrent affecting take-up of special guardianship by unrelated foster carers.

A key advantage of kinship care is perceived to lie in its 'built in inclusiveness' (Breeff, 1999). There is evidence of kinship carers having a high commitment to promoting contact, even where circumstances are difficult. However, there is also strong evidence that it can be problematic, with difficulties arising from interpersonal conflict and hostility and concerns about the ability of some carers to protect children in contact situations. In consequence, it would be a mistake to make general assumptions about how contact is likely to proceed in kinship placements (Laws, 2001).

Information collected from our survey and interviews revealed the full spectrum of contact issues, from cases where contact had been informally negotiated and was perceived to be working well through to cases where family relationships were conflicted and contact was highly problematic. In overall terms, most children were in contact with members of their

---

[54] Although we use "contact" as a shorthand term for face-to-face involvement with birth family members, it should be acknowledged that it is an awkward concept when applied to kinship care settings where the interplay of family relationships is an integral feature of placement.

birth families. Over four-fifths (84%) of the entire sample were in at least monthly contact with a relative (including contact with relatives with whom children were living), as were two-thirds (67%) of those living with unrelated foster carers.

Table 6.2 shows frequency of direct contact with relatives outside of the child's placement at the time of data collection and excludes any family members living with the child. In order to maximise the data on child contact, the table merges information collected from carers and social workers. The carer's view has been privileged where data were available from both sources.[55]

Table 6.2
Frequency of direct contact with birth family members

	At least weekly %	At least monthly %	Less often %	Never %	Number (n)
Birth mother	21	34	33	12	n = 94
Birth father	12	20	29	40	n = 91
Sibling(s)	36	18	32	14	n = 44
Grandparent(s)	24	20	20	36	n = 45
Aunts/uncles	40	17	20	23	n = 75

The findings highlight the high levels of regular contact children maintained with their siblings and extended family members. Children had regular contact with a broad range of relatives, including cousins, great-grandparents, great-aunts and uncles, stepfamily members and family friends. One child (previously adopted) had continuing letterbox contact

---

[55] Carers and social workers were asked to provide this information only for family members the child was not living with. Unfortunately, not all did so. We have adjusted for this by excluding contact data for particular relatives (for example, a grandparent) where children were known to be living with a relative of that type. The results were also affected by missing data. The findings above must therefore be seen as very much a conservative estimate of family contact external to the placement. The table relates to all children living with carers (n = 113) and not just those where a special guardianship order had been formally granted.

with her siblings and parent. Parental contact has been found to diminish over time in kinship placements and this is likely to be reflected in the relatively less frequent contact patterns for birth parents when compared to other relatives (Hunt *et al*, 2008). Loss of contact is more likely for fathers, especially if the child is placed on the maternal side of the family, and two-fifths of our children (the highest proportion for any category of relative) had no contact at all with their birth fathers at the time of data collection.

Placement of children on the maternal or paternal side of the family also affects contact patterns and birth mothers and fathers appear more likely to retain involvement with their children in kinship placements than is the case in unrelated foster care (Farmer and Moyers, 2008). Although this difference between stranger and kinship care was traceable in our data, it did not prove to be a significant finding for birth fathers. However, it did prove to be significant for birth mothers in this sample. No birth mothers had monthly or more frequent contact with children in unrelated foster care compared to 63 per cent in kinship placements, and this may reflect a tendency for special guardianship to be taken up by unrelated foster carers when mothers are no longer obviously on the scene.[56] Where birth mothers did have more frequent contact with their children, however, this was associated with children having a better overall sense of well-being; a finding that may be symptomatic of there being a tendency for greater harmony and consensus to exist in relationships surrounding the child in these cases.[57]

Carers were also asked to report whether the existing overall level of contact with relatives was about right for them and their child. As can be seen in Table 6.3, a majority of those who responded felt that it was about right irrespective of whether the contact pattern was very regular or relatively infrequent. Where carers felt that contact levels were too high, their concerns centred on the distress or confusion caused to the child, the impact of contact on their subsequent behaviour or on their manipulation by birth parents and its unsettling effect on the placement. These concerns

---

[56] Mann-Whitney U Exact Test: $p = 0.01$; $n = 90$.

[57] Kendall's tau-b test: $p = 0.05$; *tau* -0.232; $n = 75$.

were not universally applied to all family members and while some relationships were perceived as negative, others might be positive for the child or even improving. Concerns about there being too little contact derived from parents moving away, insufficient contact with siblings in other adoptive or foster placements or concerns about the impact on the child where contact was sporadic or inconsistent or where contact had been completely lost.

Table 6.3
Is the current level of birth family contact about right?

	About right %	Too much %	Too little %	Unsure %	Number (n)
Right for child	64	17	11	7	n = 70
Right for carer	59	22	8	11	n = 64

As we have seen (see Chapter 5), in the majority of cases the granting of a special guardianship order made little substantive difference to formal contact arrangements. Contact orders were made in favour of birth mothers in just over one-quarter of cases and of birth fathers in around one-fifth. Just one father was prevented contact with his child. In cases where contact orders had been made or changed (n = 25), the majority of special guardians felt that these court decisions had been taken in the best interests of the child (75%) and broadly provided the level of contact wanted by the child, at least to some degree (83%) if not completely (50%). Just two carers felt that these court-sanctioned contact arrangements had created "some degree" of risk for children during contact, although two-thirds felt that they had added to tensions between them and other birth family members.

The period subsequent to the granting of the special guardianship order had, however, seen some change in frequency of contact with birth parents. Contact patterns had remained unchanged in less than half the special guardianship cases (43% for mothers and 45% for fathers). In around one in seven cases, contact had become more frequent (14% for birth mothers, 15% for fathers), but in another two-fifths it had declined (43% for birth mothers, 40% for birth fathers). The extent to which these changes may be related to the permanency implications of special guardianship is difficult to discern from our data. It is just as likely that they reflect the passage of time and the ebb and flow of relationships that occur when children are separated from their birth parents.

As discussed earlier, where family relationships were tense and conflicted, contact had an unsettling effect on children and carers, and a negative influence on the placement and children's feelings of security and permanence. For just over one-half of the case study sample, contact arrangements were supervised by the local authority. In some instances, this role derived from the fact that birth parents lived at some distance from the child and transportation was required for visits. More commonly, however, it reflected a need for mediation and for contact to take place on neutral ground, for example, in a family centre. Contact arrangements, if they existed at all, were much less frequent for unrelated foster carers (perhaps twice yearly) than was the case for kinship carers, where monthly or more frequent contact with birth parents was quite common.

In some cases, where relationships were more harmonious, contact was informally negotiated between relative carers, children, birth parents and other family members and was seen to be proceeding reasonably well. In these scenarios, the benefits for children of feeling properly integrated within the family network could be quite evident:

> *He has the opportunity to see his mum and dad, which I believe he wouldn't have got if he had been adopted . . . He has a history. He has a story that someone can actually tell him. He has photographs of both sides of his family . . . He gets to see his extended family, which mine is quite large. He's got lots of cousins, we go to weddings, there's lots [of relatives] within a radius of a 10-minute walk.* (Great-aunt)

Where these relationships were stronger, contact tended to be more flexible and had less often required ratification by the court. The clarity provided by negotiations in advance also appeared advantageous:

[He] sees his family every other week ... and basically they left it to our discretion how these visits were going to go. They didn't even put it in the court order. (Aunt)

We suggested [to the social worker] what contact would be like, how we could arrange it. It was more like [us] coming to an agreement of how we would do [it] ... and they just wrote it in the report, because it was fine by them. (Adult cousin)

In some instances, as with this cousin, the rhythm of contact had improved and become more normalised once the local authority was no longer on the scene. It became part of the fabric of negotiated family relationships:

I think it's also because ... we haven't got social services hanging over our heads ... I wouldn't say we follow the suggested way of contact, because it's like when she's available, when I'm available ... If we go away for the week, she can come along. So it's much easier now.

Even in these generally positive cases, which formed a minority overall, progress was not always untroubled. In some instances, contact with birth parents created anxiety and could have an unsettling effect on young children:

She has a few bedwetting days and ... it's always around the time she sees her mum ... But I think they're more anxious than, you know ... She sees her once a month and then I get two or three days of naughtiness and stroppy tantrums. (Grandmother, girl four years old)

Carers generally appeared mindful of the need to manage potential risks in contact situations and this is consistent with recent findings on kinship care more generally.[58] Where parents experienced mental ill health or were

---

[58] Hunt and colleagues (2008) found little evidence of contact putting children at risk in their sample of kinship carers. Farmer and Moyers (2008) also found that carers were committed to putting the children's needs first in contact and that risks were only evident in six per cent of cases.

drug or alcohol dependent and, in consequence, their behaviour could be unpredictable, or where they associated with doubtful adults, carers seemed mindful of the need to manage contact carefully:

> *I said to [his birth mother] very recently in a review that . . . he won't be coming to stay with you until he's old enough to know right from wrong and knows how to protect himself. I don't just mean sexually . . . or physically, but that he knows . . . that he's not to keep secrets from us and things like that . . . So I'm very honest with his mum about my expectations for [him].* (Great-aunt)

In some instances, where tensions were running high, carers temporarily withheld contact until issues of concern could be discussed and clarified, sometimes utilising the local authority as mediator. In these circumstances, carers sometimes appeared uncertain about their legal rights:

> *What rights have I got to say, 'No, I'm not doing it'? She'll get her when I want her to have her, not when she thinks it feels fit for her, because she never turned up and we sat waiting and waiting and I'm not prepared to do it this time.* (Grandmother)

Established patterns of sporadic or infrequent parental contact were a major source of frustration for carers and weighed heavily on children. What seemed to matter for carers and children was less the overall frequency of contact than the quality of contact when it took place and its regularity and predictability. Where the lives of birth parents were chaotic or beset with health difficulties, this seldom seemed to occur. Where parents had been out of touch for lengthy periods or contact was limited, the attempt to renew contact caused considerable stress, especially where children were very young and had not developed a significant relationship with the parent or where they were reluctant to have the rhythm of their lives disturbed or have old (perhaps negative) memories resurface. This could put carers in an uncomfortable position where contact was expected:

> *He does get pushed into going to contact, which I'm a bit reluctant about because he doesn't know her . . . and he doesn't know*

dad . . . But they don't want to go . . . to see mum. This is the worst thing. They don't want to see her because they all said it reminds them of what happened . . . I suppose I really force them a bit, because social services say they have to go. I don't agree with it because [they are] not old enough to make their own decisions. (Unrelated foster carer, twice yearly contact order for sibling group)

It's like putting him in a room with a total stranger . . . It's not nice to see. (Paternal grandmother referring to contact with birth mother)

Most carers believed in contact and wanted to promote it, even where relationships with a parent were fraught. However, where relationships were marked by tension or outright hostility, where parents did not accept the need for placement or were unable or unwilling to work with carers, contact encounters tended to be unsettling for the children concerned and could lead to resistance:

The [supervision order] was made because the contact with [her] father is very difficult and he has supervised contact once a month . . . We wanted her to keep contact with her dad, even though he couldn't stand us . . . But the problems started when her father . . . had an outburst when he took her out because he couldn't take her back to his flat. The order had never been made for that, it would have been too confusing for her. So he had an outburst and, since that day, [she] has refused to go and see him. But, of course, he thinks that it's us stopping her. (Maternal grandmother referring to contact with birth father)

The last two quotes also hint at the divisions that can occur between different sides of the family and how these may affect parental access to children, the working relationship between parent and carer and, perhaps ultimately, the quality of the relationship with the child.[59] The dynamics of family relationships are always complicated and provide ample

---

[59] In both of these cases, contact with the birth parent on the same side of the family was perceived to be relatively unproblematic and took place frequently.

opportunity on both sides for children to receive unhelpful mixed messages. However, for contact to work well it does seem important that there is parental acceptance of the placement, a willingness to reinforce the primary role of the carer and to work with them in the interests of the child. From the carer's perspective, there needs to be a willingness to embrace contact with birth parents and other family members (which was largely the case), to understand how this may benefit the child and to negotiate even-handedly when conflicts arise. Given the complexity of family histories and dynamics in special guardianship cases, there is also (in many cases) going to be a place for ongoing social work support to mediate these relationships and facilitate contact arrangements. It is to these matters that we turn in the next chapter.

Summary

This chapter has explored the placement progress and well-being of children, the impact of special guardianship on the carer's family and issues arising from children's contact with parents and other birth family members.

Placement progress and relationships

- Most carers (76%) and social workers (83%) felt that the placements had gone "very well". Placements were perceived to have gone rather less well for boys and for children with emotional and behavioural difficulties.
- Social workers viewed the placements as "very" (81%) or "quite" (16%) suitable for the children. The safety of children was not a general concern, as most social workers reported that there were "no" (74%) or "very few" (21%) safety concerns. Where there were, their worries were generally about the potential for future risks arising from child behaviour or family contact.
- The interviews revealed the close relationships between carers and children that had grown over time. Grandparents, for example, had often had a share in the care of children from birth. Where relationships were longstanding, children had often been absorbed into the everyday rhythms of family life and felt secure and well cared for.

- Special guardianship in family settings involved a similar reordering of relationships within the family as found in kinship adoptions. Although confusing for some children, this was generally handled by carers in an open way and in terms appropriate to the child's age and understanding.
- Social workers reported high levels of commitment to the placement by carers (96%) and children (89%), but greater ambivalence from parents with only 44 per cent "fully" committed.

Child well-being

- Most children were reported to be faring quite well at the time of data collection, especially in relation to their health, attachments and emotional well-being.
- Overall well-being was significantly lower for older children, and in some respects for children with learning disabilities as well as for those living in unrelated foster care settings.
- Most children were considered healthy, but a minority had chronic health problems. Carers worried about the future psychological well-being of children where they had experienced past abuse or neglect or where families had histories of mental ill health.
- Attachment and behaviour difficulties were quite common in the present, with children described variously as withdrawn, clingy or attention seeking or presenting aggressive or defiant behaviours. These problems were often heightened before or after contact with relatives.
- School could be a difficult arena and children were considered to be faring less well in relation to education, the development of skills and interests and self-confidence than in other developmental areas.

The impact of special guardianship on carers and their families

- Most carers felt that special guardianship had given them greater control over decisions affecting the child's life (97%) and greater legal security (97%), and reduced the risk that the child could be removed by parents or local authority (91%), while enabling the child to retain a link with birth parents (74%). In these respects, the order was meeting their expectations.

- While in some cases this transition had not greatly affected the pattern of family relationships, in others it had been daunting and involved complex negotiations, especially in relation to contact.
- However, the transition had a material and psychological impact on the lives of some carers and their families. Life plans had to be adjusted, some carers had to give up employment, increasing the strain on family resources, and most sacrificed part (or all) of their social lives.

Perceptions of permanence

- The meaning of special guardianship was confusing for children and explanations were provided by carers in relatively simple terms. The legal arrangement seemed less important to children than a sense of psychological permanence: knowing that they were going to stay, that they felt safe and secure and that they were fully part of the family.
- Names seemed quite important as a means of belonging. Where a name change had not been sanctioned by the court, some children had informally hyphenated their surnames and children often expressed the need to refer to their carers as "Mum" or "Dad".
- Helping children build a sense of permanence and belonging took care over time. It was much more difficult where relationships with birth parents were conflicted and children received mixed messages about whose children they really were or how long they might stay. It is in these circumstances that the permanency limitations of special guardianship (compared to adoption) are most exposed.

Birth family contact and relationships

- Most children were in at least monthly contact with a relative. Regular frequent contact was more common with siblings and extended family members than with birth parents. Loss of contact was more likely for birth fathers rather than mothers and contact was affected by divisions between different sides of the family.
- Although there was no difference for fathers, birth mothers had

significantly less contact with children in unrelated foster care settings as compared to placement with kin. Where birth mothers did have frequent contact, this was associated with children having a better sense of overall well-being. There was very little evidence overall of risk to children during contact.

- Most carers felt that the existing level of contact (whether frequent or not) was about right. Where the level of contact was considered to be too high, concerns related to the distress or confusion experienced by the child, the impact of contact on their behaviour or the emotional manipulation of the child by birth parents.

- Contact orders had been made in favour of birth mothers in around one-quarter of cases and of birth fathers in around one-fifth. Most carers felt these court decisions had been taken in the best interests of the child (75%) and provided the level of contact wanted by the child, at least to some degree (83%), although two-thirds felt that it had added to tensions between them and other birth family members.

- Subsequent to the order, there had been a decline over time in birth parent contact in around two-fifths of cases, a pattern found more generally in kinship and foster care research.

- Carers generally had a commitment to promoting contact. Where relationships within the family were more consensual, contact had been negotiated informally, was considered to be proceeding quite well, and was of considerable benefit to children. Where relationships were conflicted or contact was sporadic and irregular, relationships were generally more fraught, children were often resistant and contact had a largely negative impact on the child and placement.

7 Supporting special guardianship

This chapter draws on evidence from the surveys and interviews to provide a focus on needs assessments and the post-order support and services provided to special guardians and their children. It considers whether, when and in what way needs assessments were undertaken and, so far as we can, the coverage of these assessments. Evidence from the policy interviews suggests that, in the main, these assessments tended to be undertaken in advance of the order being granted (see Chapter 3). As such, this section includes evidence on all children, including those not yet living with their special guardianship family. It is axiomatic that the remainder of the chapter dealing with post-order support services focuses only on those cases where a special guardianship order had been made.

Assessment of need for support and services

Local authorities do not have a legal duty to assess the support needs of all applicants seeking special guardianship. Where the child has been formally looked after immediately before application and an assessment is requested by their carer or a birth parent, the local authority is obliged to provide one. For children looked after in foster care, of course, it should be the case that the existing support package for the child can be reviewed in light of a special guardianship application.

Where the child has not been looked after, the local authority has a power to assess needs if requested by the guardian, child or another person or agency with an interest in the child (Department for Education and Skills, 2005). If the local authority refuses to conduct an assessment, it must provide written reasons and an opportunity to make representations. The assessment outcome should identify all services to be provided in the form of a written service plan. Ideally, this should occur before the court hearing and form part of the "bundle" presented to the court.

Four-fifths of our sample of 81 carers had either been offered some form of needs assessment by the local authority or had requested one (65 cases, 80%); one in ten, however, had not (eight cases, 10%).[60] Not all assessments had been completed at the conclusion of fieldwork, but this was the case for over four-fifths of these assessments (56 out of 65). In line with data from the policy interviews, there were only three cases where the needs assessment was conducted after the court hearing. Reasons for the delay associated with this small number of late assessments were not clear from the information available to us. Virtually all of the assessments had been carried out by children's services; only one had been undertaken by a local authority welfare rights service.

Furthermore, only in two cases did relative carers report that the local authority had refused an assessment once one had been requested. One case concerned a child who had left unrelated foster care to live with a grandparent; the other a child who had been living informally with a relative. In the former case, written reasons for refusal had definitely been provided and the grandparent had asked for the request to be reconsidered. In this case, she did subsequently receive some assistance with childcare costs and birth family contact after a lengthy struggle. In the other, the carer was not certain about the procedure that had been followed, but did not receive additional support beyond a monthly financial allowance. When asked to comment on how this had impacted on them and their children, the carers made the following observations on the questionnaire:

Financial difficulty in providing basic items, such as bed, clothes and other items for the child.

We could not afford a nursery place and no respite care was offered. We were led to believe that support would be there for us for up to three years.

---

[60] These data result from merging the information provided by carers and/or social workers, where only one source of information was available. Where both carers and social workers had made returns, the carer's view was privileged. The percentages reported above relate to the whole sample of carers (n = 81), although for some cases (eight) there was some missing data.

While the overall proportion that received some assessment of need was encouraging to find, many carers did not perceive the coverage of these assessments to be sufficiently comprehensive and there appeared to be plenty of scope for misinformation to exist about their support entitlements. Table 7.1 shows the breakdown of key support areas covered during the assessment process and the degree to which these areas were felt to have been covered, from the perspective of carers and social workers.

Table 7.1

Support areas covered during needs assessment: carer and social worker views

Support areas	Carer				Social worker			
	Very much so %	To some degree %	No %	(n =)	Very much so %	To some degree %	No %	(n =)
Legal assistance	34	45	21	n = 47	61	30	9	n = 54
Financial assistance	52	38	10	n = 48	83	15	2	n = 59
Other support and services	36	47	17	n = 47	75	23	2	n = 57
Help with birth family contact	40	38	21	n = 47	66	29	5	n = 56
Training/support for carer	18	40	42	n = 45	38	38	24	n = 50

Table 7.1 shows that social workers were considerably more optimistic than carers that these important areas of support had been adequately addressed during the assessment process. Only in relation to one area, financial assistance, did a bare majority of carers feel that these issues had been explored in depth, and opportunities for training seem to have been particularly ill considered. Of course, this should not imply that one narrative is right and the other wrong. As some policy interviewees had pointed out, the short time limits for assessment and preparation of court

reports meant that practitioners often had to play catch-up after the event. Equally, in the maelstrom of assessment and preparation for court some discussions may have faded into the background of carers' minds. However, given the fact that the majority of needs assessments took place prior to court, this pattern of inconsistency raises some concerns. At the very least, we can say that whatever discussions did take place were not as memorable for carers as they were for the social workers concerned.

There is no statutory obligation on local authorities to meet specific needs identified in special guardianship cases, although all local authorities do have a general duty of care, a breach of which can be challenged in the courts. In this respect, therefore, it is similar to provisions for adoption (Masson *et al*, 2008a). A completed needs assessment, therefore, did not always carry a guarantee that these services would be subsequently provided. There were several cases where carers thought that a promise had been made that certain services would be delivered, only to experience later disillusionment. In some instances, such as the case illustration provided below, financial support plans were amended even after apparent agreement had been reached with solicitors.

A sibling group of three children had been placed with their aunt and uncle for more than eight years, initially as kinship foster carers with an independent fostering agency and, more recently, as special guardians. All of these children had learning disabilities and associated emotional and behavioural difficulties. Both carers had given up employment to care for the children's needs on a full-time basis.

After their needs assessment, these carers thought agreement had been reached on an overall financial and support package which, they claim, had been approved by their solicitor. This would not involve a reduction in the allowance paid to them as foster carers. However, the support plan presented to the court had been substantially revised downwards and this was the package finally approved by the court. Not surprisingly, they felt aggrieved and frustrated with the local authority concerned, as their comments on the questionnaire suggest:

I think it is truly frustrating that the court is able to see what should be the clear way forward, but leave the local authority free to devise a scheme it chooses and expects that everyone will concur with what they say will happen. No one can be expected to make a special guardianship order for three disabled children without financial security and, having once agreed, they should not be free to go back on the agreement. We need to know we have financial security for this. Fixed payments with no annual reviews were agreed with the local authority. It was also agreed that state benefits would not be taken into account. The local authority has now gone back on the agreement and the court does not have the authority to direct it.

Post-order social work contact

There is some evidence from kinship care research that these cases tend to be closed before carers are ready to manage independently (Laws, 2001; Harwin *et al*, 2003) and that they tend to receive a lower level of service than is the case for unrelated foster carers (Farmer and Moyers, 2008). Particularly high levels of contact and support appear to be needed in the early stages of placement (Farmer and Moyers, 2008). Some social workers report that kinship carers do not always respond well to offers of support even where it is needed (Schofield *et al*, 2008), although this is not necessarily a view shared by kinship carers themselves (Broad *et al*, 2001). The policy interviews also revealed different views amongst social workers about the degree to which special guardianship families should be expected to manage independently of social work support – a view more prevalent in areas with less well-developed services (see Chapter 3).

At the point of data collection, most social workers were no longer "in touch" with families where special guardianship orders had been made (61%; n = 49). In most of these cases, case closure had occurred in the past 12 months (64%). Around one-half of the interview sample were still in touch with social workers, some formally and others informally, although a majority (11 out of 15) were continuing to receive a regular financial allowance.

Apart from financial assistance, some carers had not received further contact once the order was made. One carer had been taken aback by the abruptness of case closure, especially since she had been a kinship foster carer up to that point, while a few commented ruefully about promises that had been made but never delivered:

> *Once we'd been to court, the social worker just dropped us and we never heard from her again. I was actually quite taken aback because . . . before the final hearing she had been so full-on whenever she'd come to see us and so friendly . . . Everybody was in agreement and, as soon as it was over, we never heard from her again . . . Not even a congratulations that it's all over . . . I hope you got what you wanted or anything.* (Grandmother, former kinship foster carer of child aged 18 months)

> *When we were going through the process of assessment, they . . . said in the first six months that they [would be] in quite close contact. They weren't . . . They've not even phoned to see how we are coping.* (Aunt, child aged three)

In another instance, a case had drifted for a time before a change of social worker brought a relatively abrupt closure after a perfunctory check with the carer:

> *I've had no support from social services. Once the guardianship was given . . . I've never had any contact . . . The social worker that did the guardianship, I got a letter to say that she was ill . . . About a month after that, someone rang up who's taken over . . . She asked: 'Are you getting any money? Are you getting any support?' I said: 'No, I'm just getting the weekly allowance' . . . She said: 'I'll come back when I've looked through these files' . . . About a month afterwards she phoned and said the case is now closed. She was closing my case because she felt everything seemed to be in place and I've not heard from them again.* (Grandmother, child aged eight)

As this comment indicates, carers were not always well positioned to challenge the decisions made by social workers and, in circumstances where support had not previously been forthcoming, they simply continued to get on with the job as best they could.

A reduction in the social work role had sometimes occurred in more propitious circumstances. Not all kinship carers had wanted or anticipated continuing support, and self-reliance (chosen or enforced) was a consistent theme in interviews. Where the child had previously been fostered, the transition to special guardianship sometimes denoted a reordering of relationships with children's services and greater freedom from the restrictions that "care" imposes on children and foster carers. In these circumstances, the process of normalising family relationships took precedence over the presence of social workers in their lives:

I think we just wanted it to be normal... as normal as it can be... We wouldn't ask for any help... so we wouldn't expect any. (Unrelated foster carer)

I preferred it to be honest and that's what I worked towards... Although it was their job to come round every six or eight weeks, it felt as if it was not natural because it was not everyday life... Having to deal with [social workers], although that was fine, I had a good relationship with them, it was still part of my life that was taken up... going through assessments, filling out forms for money, chasing them up when they didn't pay me... I just wanted to get back to my life I had before, bringing up my children, going about my life... not having social workers on the phone. (Great-aunt, child aged six)

As this last comment suggests, many kinship carers do not choose to be foster carers, rather they are generally thrust into it as a result of family circumstances. Many do not want to be perceived as "mainstream" foster carers and, although they may need and appreciate support when it is provided (as this carer did in relation to supervised contact), there is greater scope for them to have ambivalent feelings about the place of social workers in their lives (Hunt, 2001; Farmer and Moyers, 2008).

Where continuing social work contact and support had been provided, it had tended to be more intensive in the early period after the order had been granted. This provided an opportunity to help the family settle down, regularise financial payments, supervise family contact where needed, identify any longer-term needs and co-ordinate access to mainstream or specialist services. Once these tasks had been completed, support tended to decline and was more reactive, dependent on requests made by carers. Supervision orders attached to special guardianship were sometimes thought necessary to guarantee access to support and services during this early period. Some carers expressed very positive views about the social workers they had contact with:

They've been remarkable throughout . . . When I first got the guardianship, they visited me weekly, then fortnightly, then monthly and then periodically . . . if I had any questions . . . Obviously I had a supervision order and they used to take her to see her mum for me, so I didn't have to go. I do it myself now. (Grandmother, child aged four)

I mean all the social workers that [he] had, and we did have a few over the years, the majority of them were very nice, and the last one he had was an absolutely terrific man. He and I . . . still keep in touch . . . every so often. (Grandmother, child aged 10)

Continuing low-key reassurance was important, as was a feeling that carers knew where to turn for help if later problems emerged. Where past experiences of support had not been particularly positive, however, worries about whether services that had been promised would be delivered in the future were at the forefront of carers' minds:

I mean we don't really get any support now . . . none whatsoever . . . I would say in the future if I need support . . . with them when they get into the teenage years and I'm pulling my hair out . . . I'm hoping social services will give me a little bit of support . . . They have promised me, but I'm hoping they will carry on. (Unrelated foster carer caring for a sibling group)

Financial assistance

Concerns about the financial implications of caring for children, as our policy interviews have shown, have acted as a deterrent for unrelated foster carers taking up custodianship and, more recently, special guardianship (Bullard *et al*, 1991; Hall, 2008; Schofield *et al*, 2008). Finance is also a serious concern for kinship carers, who have often received lower allowances than unrelated foster carers (Waterhouse and Brocklesby, 1999; Broad, 2007), and who may feel reluctant to ask for or simply not expect help. In this respect, the Munby judgment does not seem to have led to a complete equalisation of allowances between kin and non-kin foster carers (Farmer and Moyers, 2008).[61] However, it is to be hoped that the Lewisham judgment will help to raise over time the level and consistency of special guardianship allowances.[62]

The powers available to local authorities with respect to financial assistance are considerable, including payment of regular allowances, one-off settling-in grants and assistance with accommodation, legal or transport costs or to meet the specific care needs of the child. Although financial allowances are generally subject to means testing and annual financial review, and should not allow for an element of remuneration, payments to foster carers are protected for a transitional period of two years after an order is made. Consistent with the Lewisham judgment, the guidance also encourages local authorities to benchmark allowances against the fostering allowance that would have been payable if the child had been fostered (Department for Education and Skills, 2005).

Hunt and colleagues' (2008) study of kinship carers found that 88 per cent were receiving some form of ongoing financial support from local authorities after the end of care proceedings. This is consistent with our survey findings on special guardianship, as can be seen in Table 7.2.[63]

---

[61] *R. (ota) L. v Manchester City Council* [2002] (cited in Farmer and Moyers, 2008, p. 221).

[62] *B v London Borough of Lewisham* [2008] EWHC 738 (Admin).

[63] This table merges information from carers and social workers in order to maximise the overall data available. Where both sources were available for a case, the guardian's view has been privileged. It only includes cases where a special guardianship order had been made.

Table 7.2
Post-order financial support

Type of support	Yes %	Not needed %	No %	(n =) %
Regular financial allowance	90	6	4	n = 69
One-off payment	48	41	12	n = 61
Assistance with legal costs	50	36	14	n = 58
Other financial help	31	55	14	n = 51

The vast majority of carers were in receipt of a regular allowance. Those that were not generally had an income level above the threshold, although this did not always mean that they were able to provide care without some financial strain on them and their families. Overall, one-half had received assistance with legal fees and smaller proportions had received other forms of financial help. "One-off payments" included settling-in grants of varying amounts, but in one case included the purchase of a larger car for a sibling group and, in another, assistance to move to a larger house. "Other help" generally included ongoing help with nursery or childminding fees or with the associated costs of birth family contact.

Although a desire for permanence, legal security and parental control had been the primary motivating factors in carers seeking special guardianship, the potential for continuing financial assistance and other support services had been a very important factor in nearly one-half of the cases surveyed. This was especially the case for those who were unemployed or who had given up employment in order to care for their children. The importance of having financial security for the child or sibling group was a major consideration:

The positives are ... having the financial support; knowing that we can give [her] everything financially. We know we can give her everything in terms of ... love and security, but it's knowing we're going to be able to provide for her financially as well ... That was a very big positive. (Unrelated foster carer)

Overall, most carers in the interview sample had obtained a regular allowance (11 out of 15). Obtaining an allowance, however, was not always straightforward. Most financial packages had been clearly agreed ahead of the court hearing and were subsequently adhered to. Others required mediation from the courts or other professionals, such as solicitors or social workers advocating for their clients, to obtain a satisfactory outcome:

> *Well, they [the court] turned round and told them to go back and sort it, because the [local authority] said they could only give us so much. The [court] said, we know you can give her more, we suggest you go back to your finance department and sort it out now. They got quite angry with them . . . What they did, whereas I'd never had an allowance for [my other child] under a residence order, they've given me an allowance for him.* (Grandmother, former kinship foster carer)

In line with data from the policy interviews (see Chapter 3), there was evidence of variation in how local authorities approached the payment of allowances in different types of cases. Where carers had previously been foster carers (unrelated or kinship), it was more likely that allowances would be subsequently protected, some for the duration of placement, others for the minimum two-year period. Many carers were still worse off, since they were subject to an annual means test and important fringe benefits, like holiday and birthday money or school clothes allowances, were no longer routinely paid. Greater variability existed in cases involving "informal" kinship carers, those not previously foster carers for the local authority. In some areas with more consistent policies, they received the same standard allowance as other carers. In others, there was evidence of a reluctance to pay. In one case, no allowance had been paid and no explanation had apparently been given. In another, the attitude of the local authority had been to put the carer off enquiring further and this had affected the likelihood that she would seek other help in the future:

> A: *They [the local authority] really downplayed that part of it . . . Of course, the solicitors that were working on our behalf in the court, they were paid for, but everything else they basically said is going to be means tested and we wouldn't qualify, so don't bother.*

Q: *And would you feel comfortable approaching them and asking for support?*

A: *I can do that, yes, it's just the last time . . . we were really dismissed altogether. I don't feel very positive about . . . getting any results really.* (Aunt)

Across all types of case there was evidence in some local authorities of attempts to negotiate allowances downwards. In these circumstances, carers were reliant on solicitors or, as above, the court to find a more satisfactory solution. In one case, this had taken a full year and engagement of a new solicitor to resolve after the local authority had resisted meeting the terms of the support plan agreed in court.

As Table 7.2 showed, around one-half of those surveyed had received additional or one-off payments. In most instances, the sums involved were likely to have been relatively small, although settling-in grants or help with childcare costs could make a substantial difference to the overall resources of carers. One interviewee, for example, had received a grant of £600 that had helped her buy most of the essential items needed for her child to move in. There were very few examples of carers receiving sizeable sums for cars or house extensions, although there were a few examples of social workers helping families to move to larger accommodation. Just two interviewees, each caring for sibling groups and with children of their own, had received assistance to buy larger cars so that they could all travel together as a family. In one of these cases, it had taken 18 months and persistent lobbying by her social worker to achieve it. Furthermore, this carer had incurred a high level of indebtedness by extending her own house to accommodate all six children without assistance from the local authority.

There was, therefore, very little evidence of carers pressing local authorities for extra resources (Hunt, 2003; see also Hunt *et al*, 2008). In early cases, there was often confusion amongst social workers and carers as to what forms of assistance might be permissible. The process of application often involved hoops and hurdles that some carers wanted to avoid. There was also a tendency for some carers to feel reluctant to ask, either because they felt they should be able to manage independently or through concern that they might be perceived as not coping:

> *Obviously, when he was on a care order, I got money for him and some of that was hard to get out of the local authority . . . I would ask for help . . . I didn't have a problem with that, but maybe other people might feel . . . they wouldn't want to ask because it would seem as if they couldn't cope . . . I think there [is a] need to look into this means testing thing because I think there should be at least a basic band of money that somebody should get, even if it's just help with holidays . . . or school uniforms . . . because it just seems that if you get on in life, you can't get anything.* (Great-aunt)

Around one-half of the survey sample had also received some help with legal fees. This was also the case for two-thirds of the interview sample. In some of these cases, where carers were not working or had given up employment to provide care, they had been eligible for legal aid. In others, the fees were met by the local authority concerned. However, there were also examples where local authorities had only agreed to pay after a lengthy period of struggle with solicitors and/or children's guardians. Where the income of some carers was above the threshold for legal aid, they attended court unrepresented and could be left confused by the proceedings:

> *I didn't have any legal support . . . My solicitor . . . pointed out that with me working now, I wouldn't get legal aid and I would have to pay . . . I wasn't represented in the court . . . I just went around and sat at the back and listened . . . Occasionally somebody might say: 'Do you understand what's going on?' . . . So it was just a great experience.* (Adult cousin)

These examples of the difficulties encountered by carers highlight the patchiness of present provision and the need for local authorities to develop more consistent policies and procedures to support financially the care of children in family settings. In a context of resource constraint, it is understandable that local authorities would seek to conserve resources and set realistic service boundaries. The policy interviews drew attention to the growing resource strain that is arising from the increase in special guardianship applications and the impact this may have on service quality. Other recent work has also indicated that only a small minority of local authorities may be able to sustain financial support packages equivalent to that which local authority foster carers receive for the duration of a child's placement (Schofield et al, 2008).

While the overall findings are encouraging, certainly when compared to the financial inconsistencies associated with residence orders, special guardianship is unlikely to fulfil its potential unless carers and their families are given a sufficient degree of financial assistance to enable them to plan for the care of their children with confidence. Their demands are generally not unreasonable. Without some degree of equivalence to fostering, it is most unlikely that unrelated foster carers will relinquish their fostering role in significant numbers, even if other aspects of special guardianship are attractive. It is also likely that kinship carers will continue to experience disadvantage and some hardship when attempting to meet their obligations to children within the family network.

Support services for the carer and/or child

Although special guardians, like adopters, have no legal entitlement to receive specific services, the guidance and regulations place a clear duty on local authorities to develop a framework for delivering post-order services (Department for Education and Skills, 2005). The policy inter-views and documents revealed considerable variation between local authorities in the range and duration of services that were provided. Areas that had developed greater early momentum and, in response to rising demand, invested in specialist social work teams (dedicated special guardianship, kinship or post-adoption teams) tended to have developed a more comprehensive range of services. In areas where this investment had not been made or where demand was low, services tended to be more residual. In some areas, apart from finance, the potential range of services on offer were considerable and included allocated support workers, access to groups and training, respite and CAMHS (Child and Adolescent Mental Health Services), supervision of birth family contact and assistance with access to mainstream welfare rights, health and education services. In some areas, these services were available to all special guardians. In others areas, access appeared to be more restricted, in the main to cases where children had been looked after or had been in care proceedings, or access to services was managed entirely on a child "in need" basis through the duty system.

Support and services overview

This continuum of services was apparent in responses to the survey. Table 7.3 identifies the range of services accessed by carers, whether they were perceived to have been helpful or unhelpful and, if they had not been accessed, whether that was because they were not considered to have been necessary or were unavailable. In order to maximise the data available, we have merged the information collected from carers and social workers. Where information was available from both a carer and a social worker for a particular case, the carer's view has been prioritised. However, it should be acknowledged that, just as we found in relation to assessment of need, social workers tended to have a more positive view of service provision than did carers. Therefore, although we have attempted to privilege the carer perspective, the findings are likely to represent an overestimate of services received.[64] Having said this, the findings do allow some quite distinctive themes and issues to emerge.

First, the table highlights some of the priority support needs of special guardians. In particular, it shows the value of reliable information, advice and guidance to help carers steer a course through the process of becoming special guardians and to help them access a range of mainstream services that are of importance for their and their children's well-being. It highlights the support needs arising from the management of often complex birth family relationships and, finally, gives emphasis to

---

[64] It was not possible to estimate reliably the degree of variance in carer and social worker views owing to the very small numbers in some cells. A visual inspection of the separated data suggested that, while social workers were more inclined to say a service had been offered or provided, carers were more likely to report that the same service had not been needed. There was little difference in responses with respect to service availability. Only carers had felt that services had not been helpful.

Table 7.3
Post-order access to support services[65]

Type of support	Yes, helpful %	Yes, but not helpful %	Not needed %	Not offered or available %	(n =)
Advice, information, guidance	76	3	12	9	n = 66
Help with childcare	16	0	59	25	n = 56
Out-of-hours service	21	2	63	14	n = 57
Respite/short breaks service	6	2	71	21	n = 52
Support groups for guardian	32	4	42	22	n = 50
Counselling for guardian	13	4	66	17	n = 53
To manage birth family contact	57	4	35	3	n = 68
To understand/manage child's behaviour	52	3	3	88	n = 66
To support child's education	33	3	62	2	n = 61
Counselling/treatment for child	34	3	58	5	n = 62
Support groups/ activities for child	26	3	53	17	n = 58

[65] Table 7.3 only includes cases where the child was living with the carer and where a special guardianship order had been granted. The variables were also affected by missing data.

the concerns of carers about how best to understand and manage the quite persistent difficult behaviour of children and, linked to this, the value of therapeutic input and support at school. Apart from financial security and costs of childcare, these appeared to be the areas that troubled carers most and were the areas where support was found helpful. These were quite closely followed by the need for support groups, training workshops and social activities for them and their children.

Second, the table indicates the presence of a core strand of self-reliance amongst carers – and this strand would have been even stronger if a carer-only perspective had been presented. Only in relation to some of the priority support areas above did a majority report that support had been absolutely necessary. Many carers wanted or expected only a minimal dependence on the local authority and, as will be seen below, many preferred to rely on support available from within their own social networks.

Third, and in a context of service variability, the evidence that services were simply not offered or not available locally was less strong than might have been anticipated.

Therapeutic support

Chapter 6 drew attention to the complex and challenging behaviour presented by many children, often arising from psychological and emotional legacies of the past. While some children appeared relatively easy to care for, others were not. Hunt and colleagues' (2008) research on kinship care found that around one-third of children (34%) in their sample were receiving some form of specialist intervention, most commonly through mental health professionals. This corresponds closely with our finding that 34 per cent of children had received or were continuing to receive individual counselling or treatment (Table 7.3). Farmer and Moyers (2008) also found little difference in the proportions of children in kinship or unrelated foster care accessing mental health services or school support through the statementing process.

The survey data suggest that most mental health services for children were accessed through the local CAMHS (Child and Adolescent Mental Health Services). At least one in five children overall had involvement with CAMHS and this had been the case for just over one-quarter of children in the interview sample. One or two other children had accessed therapeutic support through educational psychologists in school settings and, as we have seen, statementing had proved helpful in securing resources of this kind. In addition, two carers had received support from psychologists to help them to work through past experiences with their children.

In general, therapeutic help was focused on the behavioural consequences of past maltreatment. In some cases, children had received psychiatric assessments or periods of brief therapy. In others, there was evidence of longer-term counselling or, for younger children, of using play therapy to unlock and understand their anger and aggression. Not all children were comfortable with this kind of support. Some dropped out quickly and not all carers felt that the support that was available was necessarily appropriate for the needs of their children. In some cases, access to CAMHS had been reinforced by sanction of the court as part of the support plan or had been included as part of the requirement attached to a supervision order. Without this authority, it may have been more difficult to access these services.

Training and support groups for guardians

Help to understand and manage the behaviour of children may also be provided through training courses, workshops or more informally through support groups. These may also have the effect of reducing isolation and enabling carers to develop networks of informal support. Several of our local authorities had provision for support groups and training, newsletters and social events. It was less often the case that these were targeted specifically at special guardians, although space was made for them to attend existing groups for adopters and foster carers.

Table 7.1 showed that training needs were one of the least well-considered areas during the assessment process. Fewer than one in five carers felt that their needs had been covered in depth and one-quarter of social workers and over two-fifths of carers reported that training had not been addressed at all. Table 7.3 shows that just over one-third of carers had attended a support group, although not all had found the experience helpful, but more than one in five had not been offered this service.

Two in five interviewees discussed their need for or experience of formal or informal training. In all cases, their concern centred on how to understand or manage in more effective ways behaviour in their children that was confusing to them. Most did not recount positive experiences. In some instances they discussed the lack of these services, even where they had been discussed at assessment:

When we were going through the assessment, they gave us a big folder. They said once it's all gone through you can pick out what courses you want, and there were a lot of different courses ... I've never seen it again ... They've never offered us any courses for difficult behaviour or anything again. (Unrelated foster carer)

Foster carers tend to get a lot of input from the local authority, but I think with special guardianship people are, in a way, left to their own devices. (Great-aunt, former kinship foster carer)

Another carer recounted a stop-and-start experience, where they were invited to a kinship group that didn't then meet regularly. Only one carer provided a favourable comment about their attendance at parenting classes. He felt these had greatly improved his ability to relate to the sibling group in his care and to understand the differences in caring for them when compared to his own birth children.

Although many of those surveyed who had attended training or support groups would probably have reported more positive experiences, the findings as a whole point to the patchy nature of this provision and to the enduring need for support to help carers manage quite complex childcare issues. The findings are also consistent with research on kinship care that suggests that kinship carers are less likely than unrelated foster carers to access training or support groups (Farmer and Moyers, 2008).

Respite

As Table 7.3 showed, very few special guardians had experience of using a respite or short breaks service, although one-fifth had never been offered a service of this kind locally. Most preferred, where feasible, to draw on resources within their own network of family and friends. However, the presence of these resources cannot be assumed, since they are the product of private systems of obligation that are negotiated within families and highly dependent on the quality of family relationships (Finch, 1989). The balance in these frequently volatile relationships may also change over time, suggesting the need for social workers to remain vigilant to these shifting dynamics.

Only four interviewees commented directly about respite arrangements, although it did emerge – alongside financial security, therapeutic support, training and consistent support from link workers – as a significant area in which needs had gone unmet. Only one carer reported having a satisfactory monthly arrangement that provided some relief from caring for a sibling group. In two cases, respite arrangements had been discussed at assessment but had never been formalised in the support plan or subsequently offered. In the fourth, a request for respite had been made but the carer was subsequently told that there were no resources to fund it:

> *It's just the support isn't there ... They said there'll be respite care ... Once a week you can have childcare if you want to go out ... We were told that if we wanted to go on holiday ... for a couple of days break, we could get respite ... There's been no suggestion of anything since that.* (Aunt)

> *They did say that there would be respite care ... I did ask once, she'd only been with me a couple of months and I was tired because ... she was up at five in the morning and then she was awake all day ... I did ask for a bit of support, but there wasn't funding so I didn't get it.* (Grandmother aged 47, child aged two years at placement)

The last comment also hints at the hesitancy carers frequently feel about asking for help of this kind. An explanation was felt to be necessary to convince the interviewer that the request was genuine and that it wasn't symptomatic of a broader inability to cope. It also signifies that, once rebuffed, there is likely to be a general reluctance to seek help again. This was, in fact, a quite common reaction amongst carers when an appeal for assistance had gone unheeded and it is something that social workers ought to bear in mind.

Birth family relationships

Chapter 6 identified contact and relationships between family members as a complex and frequently conflicted arena. Children had high levels of contact with relatives outside the placement and contact frequency was considerably higher for children in kinship placements, although there was evidence of a decline in frequency of birth parent contact over time.

Chapter 3 revealed, from a practitioner perspective, the high level of demand for support and mediation around family contact, the frequency of contact sanctioned by the courts when compared to parental contact in adoption cases, and the resource implications of providing these services over long periods of time. The responsibility for self-managing these relationships was also considered to be a considerable barrier affecting take-up of special guardianship by unrelated foster carers.

Table 7.3 showed that six in ten special guardians had received some support with birth family contact, although a few had found this unhelpful. In just over one-third of cases, this support had not been considered necessary and it was very rare for it to be completely unavailable. For almost one in ten special guardianship orders made, the courts had also attached supervision orders. These generally covered the first year and were often used to guarantee that local authorities would put resources in place to support special guardians, frequently where contact difficulties were anticipated.

In this context, for just over one-half of the interview sample, local authorities had supervised the contact arrangements between children and their birth parents, at least for a period of time. Generally this occurred where carers were reluctant to meet birth parents directly, where relationships were highly conflicted or where the relationship between carer and birth parent was relatively weak. In these circumstances, provision of a neutral venue and a social work presence during contact was a relief to carers and reduced their anxiety for their children:

I didn't want to get into big discussions about everything, so it was decided that her contact would be in a family centre and it would be supervised by one of the . . . adoption support team . . . We've had a consistent member of staff, because that was an issue for me . . . There had been different people turning up (who) *he never knew and, because of his background, how he came into care and all the moves he had before and during care, it was very important that he had stability . . . It was the same contact centre and . . . after a while that improved.* (Unrelated foster carer)

The mediation role played by some social workers was also valued, especially in periods when tensions were running high and carers were reluctant to honour contact arrangements, but also to help birth parents adjust their expectations, their approach to contact or the messages they gave to children. Their presence was also important where birth parents were seeking to renew contact after a lengthy absence or where contact had been highly erratic and upsetting for the children concerned. Although carers sometimes had to assert themselves to manage their own social workers, the role of social workers as brokers could be helpful:

Since 2005 he's seen [his birth mother] twice and now . . . she wants access . . . At the moment [children's services] are asking me to contact mum by phone and I said: 'No, it has to be in person, not by phone' . . . I want to see her commitment to [him] before I let her see him, because it destroyed him the last time. I built him up and built him up, not because I was asked to, because I believe his mum is his mum and his family is his family. I was building him up and every time I was coming home with him so angry . . . It was an awful sight . . . I not only had to calm him down but try to get him to understand . . . It got to the stage where I was fed up. (Unrelated foster carer)

Despite the difficulties associated with this case, it tends to foreground the continuing commitment shared by many carers about the value of contact with birth parents, where it is positive for the children concerned, and also the ongoing support that is likely to be necessary to help carers manage these relationships productively for their children.

Contingency plans

Social workers responding to the survey were asked to identify whether contingency plans had been drawn up against the risk that one-off crises or longer-term difficulties might arise in the future. As we have seen, some carers were concerned and wanted reassurance that, should difficulties emerge at a later stage, they would have a route back into services. Of those who responded (n = 63), two-thirds (65%) reported that this was the case. However, in more than one-third of cases (35%), planning of this kind had either not been undertaken or the existence of these plans were unknown to the social worker concerned.

Where evidence of contingency planning had been evident, some social workers simply made reference to service plans drawn up at the assessment stage taking account of future events. Others suggested an alternative placement would be found if events subsequently proved too difficult for the child. However, most social workers were more specific and their responses clustered into three broadly equal groups. First, there were those who suggested that families had been made aware that they could access help through the duty system, implying that further assessments would then be undertaken to see if additional services were needed or warranted.

> The guardian is aware that they can contact family services for a support plan assessment and advice.

> The guardian would make a referral to social services for a review of the support plan.

> No, although the guardian is aware that they could refer back to the local authority for further assessment if needed.

It is helpful for guardians to be signposted in this way, so that they are provided with a clear pathway to further assessments. However, from the material that has been presented, it is clear that this also involves significant barriers for guardians and, in circumstances where an initial approach is met with an unhelpful response from social workers not known to them, guardians are likely to feel disillusioned quite quickly.

A second cluster of responses centred on the presence of support from family and friends. These responses implied that the future needs of guardians were likely to be well met from within their own social network. In some cases, there was evidence that these arrangements had been well planned and that those who may step in to provide care in emergencies had themselves been assessed. In other cases, these arrangements seemed more uncertain, based more on assumptions about the willingness of family members to help out.

> The guardian's best friend is herself a long-term foster carer. She is committed to caring for the child should ill health or other crises affect the placement. The child has known this person since she was a baby and visits now once a month. This "back-up" carer was part of our special guardianship order recommendations.

> Her sister was named as a carer to enable the grandparents some respite and would be prepared to care for the young person should the placement break down.

> The guardian's support network is to be involved.

The final group of responses was linked to the presence of dedicated post-order support teams. These teams were organised in different ways, although they generally provided allocated social work support, at least during the early post-order phase. As we saw in Chapter 3, they were more likely to have a menu of services available to guardians (including support groups and training) and to use newsletters and social activities as a means of keeping in touch with guardians who were registered with them. Strategies of this kind are likely to make it easier for guardians to return for help when times are difficult, even if they have not previously availed themselves of the services on offer.

> We are now staffed to make an annual review of support plans, which should manage changes and keep guardians connected to the support services we offer.

> The kinship care team can be contacted by the grandparents for any assistance and support they need.

Not all carers will want access to support services. Many will prefer to rely on their own networks of support. However, it is important to make access to support as easy as it can be. Most carers appreciate clear information, advice and signposting, preferably to workers they know. Many guardians also need to be reassured that difficulties are to be expected and that an approach for help will not be read as a symptom of failure. The development of informal strategies to maintain links with guardians can help to achieve a sustainable balance between the self-reliance that many guardians emphasise and an approachable port of call when particular support is needed.

Informal support

The presence of informal support networks is one of the factors that act as a buffer for adults against adverse life experiences (Kelly *et al*, 2000). A close relationship with a parent or principal carer, a supportive extended family, friendship networks and positive school experiences have also been identified as resilience-promoting factors in the environments of children and young people (Newman and Blackburn, 2002). Hunt and colleagues' (2008) research found that most kinship carers (81 per cent) reported that their families and friends were supportive of the placement, although the support they provided was more often emotional and occasional rather than practical and regular. One-third reported receiving no practical help from these quarters.

Two-thirds of our interview sample discussed aspects of the support they received from family and friends. Some emphasised its importance to them, as much for the emotional and moral support that close relationships offered as for the practical help that was provided. However, especially where support from children's services was weaker, assistance with childcare, respite and the purchase of essential items for the child could be quite critical:

I've got loads of support . . . It's excellent, yes . . . It's just as well because I didn't get anything from social services. (Grandmother)

We are really close with my mum . . . She does the school runs for [her] . . . She absolutely adores my mum . . . She goes down to my sister's, which is just round the corner and she'll overnight there with them. (Unrelated foster carer)

I do have what I call "me-me" days where my mum will come in and she will have her for a night and I'll have a night out with the girls here and there ... I don't go out every week. I suppose for me once every three months is quite a treat. (Grandmother)

Locality was important. As the middle comment implies, support was easier to mobilise when extended family members and friends lived close by. Occasionally, carers were also able to draw on advice and information from friends and acquaintances who worked in the caring professions or to share experiences with others in the neighbourhood who had taken on similar roles. These had proved to be valuable connections:

I have had good support from her mum's school friend. We've kept in touch and she has done social work ... During that time she used to ring me about twice a week and ask me how it was going and advise me. So that was a great help. (Grandmother)

I have a friend. I've seen her recently. If I ever feel down I get on a bus and go and see her ... We've both been through the same things and we can get on and talk about it and have a cry together. (Grandmother)

However, it was also the case that these support networks could be fragile. Family members sometimes fell out and support was withdrawn for periods of time or, despite initial good intentions, support that was promised was never delivered. Furthermore, where family relationships were conflicted, the decision to proceed with special guardianship could result in the loss of support and goodwill from family members. In these circumstances, carers were often left to go it alone:

When I took this on, none of us knew about the payments, because while I had her, there were no payments during that time ... So when everything was going through the assessment process and they said I was suitable, [the social worker] started going through what it entails, and all the family was there at the family conference. So everybody suddenly decided they wanted her. And because of that I stopped getting support [from them]. The relief that I could get from babysitting, it all stopped. (Cousin)

To be honest, I could really do with a little respite. At first, her paternal grandmother was promising the earth, and the dad . . . They said they would support us . . . I said to her, if you could just have her overnight once a month, it would help me out. She did it the two months . . . but the third month when I went to take her, she had moved house and never told us. (Aunt)

Respite was a genuine need for carers, even for a couple of hours at a time. However, establishing sufficient trust to be able to leave children with other than one or two immediate family members was an issue for some carers. Alongside the question of confidence was a concern about burdening others and this engendered a reluctance to ask:

I don't like to leave them with people . . . I know it sounds corny, doesn't it? I don't like to think that I'm putting on anybody, so that's why it's just my mum . . . Apart from that, I don't like to think that anybody else would be looking after her, to be honest. (Grandmother, caring for two siblings)

Overall, the findings raise questions about whether initial assessments of the potential for support within the network of family and friends are sufficient unless the dynamics within these relationships continue to be monitored. Respite services, for example, may not be considered necessary at the outset, but the situation may change quite significantly over the course of time. Assumptions about the degree of informal support that is likely to accrue might well be misplaced and this may require support plans to be revisited. The volatility of many family relationships therefore reinforces the need to provide carers with clear routes back into professional support and services should this network fail, not least because a build-up of stress may ultimately affect the quality of care given to the child and potential stability of the placement.

Summary

This chapter has examined the process of assessing the support needs of special guardianship applicants and the post-order support and services that were provided.

Assessment of need

- Most carers (80%) had been provided with some assessment of their support needs; at least 10 per cent had not. Almost all assessments were conducted before the court hearing and were conducted by local authority social workers. In only two cases had an assessment been refused.
- The coverage of these assessments was variable. Only in one area, financial assistance, did a majority of carers (52%) feel that their needs had been covered in considerable depth. Training needs were particularly ill considered. Needs that were identified and agreed did not always subsequently translate into discrete services.

Post-order social work contact

- At the point of data collection, most social workers were no longer in touch with special guardianship families (61%). In most cases, case closure had occurred in the past 12 months (64%).
- For some carers, case closure had been abrupt and all contact had ceased immediately after the court hearing. Others had expected a continuing link, but became quite quickly disillusioned.
- Not all case closures were unwelcome. Not all carers wanted or expected further support, beyond financial assistance, and self-reliance was a consistent theme in interviews. Some ex-foster carers (unrelated and kinship) saw the normalisation of family relationships and routines as part of the attraction of special guardianship.
- Where social work contact continued, it tended to be more intensive in the early post-order phase to help the family settle, supervise family contact and co-ordinate access to other services. Contact then registered in a lower key and was more dependent on carers seeking further help. Supervision orders were sometimes used by the courts to ensure access to services in this early period.

Financial assistance

- Although provision of financial assistance is discretionary, the powers available to local authorities are quite comprehensive. Allowances are only protected for foster carers for a period of two years, although they may be guaranteed for duration of placement.
- The vast majority of special guardians (90 per cent) were in receipt of a regular allowance. One-half had received assistance with legal fees and smaller proportions had received other financial help. Although not amongst the primary motivating factors for seeking an order, the potential for financial assistance had been a very important consideration in almost one-half of the cases.
- Obtaining an allowance was often not straightforward. Most financial packages had been agreed ahead of court and were then honoured; others were not and were subject to court directive or protracted negotiations through solicitors.
- There was also evidence of variation between local authorities in their approach to financial assistance. Allowances were more likely to be protected for foster carers – some for the minimum two-year period, others for the duration of placement. Many carers were still worse off, since they were subject to means tests and fringe benefits had been removed. Greatest variation was apparent for "informal" kinship carers and those not previously known to children's services. Across all cases, there was also evidence in some local authorities of attempts to negotiate allowances downwards.
- There was little evidence of carers pressing for extra resources. Indeed, some were reluctant to seek help out of concern they would be perceived as not coping. Others did not expect further assistance. A more consistent framework of guaranteed payments is needed to enable carers to plan care with greater certainty. Without this certainty, take-up, especially by unrelated foster carers, is likely to remain limited and some kinship carers will continue to face hardship.

Other support services

The survey findings highlighted the uneven development of support services across local authorities, but also some key areas of need, in particular:

- Reliable advice, information and guidance is needed at all stages.
- There is a need for help in managing complex and often volatile family relationships. Six in ten special guardians had required some support with birth family contact (61%) and it was very rare for help in this area to be unavailable. For just over one-half of the interview sample, contact arrangements were directly supervised by the local authority.
- Therapeutic input and support are needed to help carers understand and manage difficult behaviour in children. Around one-third of children (34%) had or were continuing to receive specialist interventions, most commonly through CAMHS, and mainly focused on the behavioural consequences of past maltreatment.
- There is a need for associated training and group-based support. Training needs had been the least well-covered area during assessment. Around one-third of carers (32%) had attended a support group, although these were rarely targeted specifically at special guardians.
- Very few carers had accessed a respite or short breaks service (six per cent). Most preferred, where feasible, to draw on resources within their own informal networks, although in one-fifth of cases (21%) this support had simply not been available.
- Two-thirds of social workers (65%) considered that contingency plans had been put in place to meet anticipated difficulties in the future. These plans included access to duty teams, reliance on informal support systems within the family or connections with dedicated support teams. The latter had a broader range of informal strategies for staying in touch with carers that would make access to future support easier.

Informal support

- The presence of informal networks of support was important for the emotional, financial and practical support they provided, especially where professional services were weak. However, the availability of this support cannot be assumed and, over time, is as likely to weaken as it is to strengthen, leaving carers more isolated. Carers also worried about burdening others and leaving children with adults, despite the need for a break.

- The strength of these networks, therefore, needs to be monitored over time and support plans may need to be adjusted in light of changing dynamics in the structure of relationships with families and friends. Assumptions made about the degree of informal support available may be misplaced and clear routes back into professional services are likely to be required.

8 Comparing children in the special guardianship sample to those in other permanent placements

This research on special guardianship was commissioned as part of a wider study of pathways and outcomes for children in three main forms of permanent placement – long-term fostering, adoption by carers and adoption by strangers (see Biehal *et al*, 2010, for details of study design). The two strands of research were therefore conducted in the same local authorities, although an additional authority was recruited to the special guardianship component to boost the size of our survey sample. This provided an opportunity to make some basic comparisons between the characteristics and circumstances of children entering special guardianship families with those of children living in these other permanent placement settings. This is the focus of this chapter.

Although these comparisons are of considerable interest, we need to be aware of the limitations attached to them. The special guardianship research comprises a study of *applications* for special guardianship although, as we have seen, two-thirds of the children (65%) had been living with their carers for two or more years at the point of data collection. In contrast, the permanent placements component is a *follow-up study* of 196 children who had been looked after in foster care in 1998 or 1999 and who were then followed up through questionnaires to carers and social workers approximately seven years later.

With respect to the general profile of looked after children, these 196 children were a highly stable group, since all of these children had remained with the same foster carers for at least three years or had moved on to adoption. It was inevitable that, over the course of seven years, some would have subsequently changed placements. However, the statistics used for comparison in this chapter are those for children who had remained with the same foster carers throughout (n = 63) and for those who were settled with adoptive families at follow-up. We cannot, of course, know whether the children in the special guardianship families will go on to experience similar levels of stability, although a pathways and outcomes study to assess both the well-being and stability of children over time will be needed to gauge adequately the potential of special guardianship to deliver permanence for children.

It would be of particular interest to make comparisons between the children who were the subject of special guardianship applications and those on residence orders, who were included in our follow-up study. However, the number of children on residence orders was very small (n = 15). Also, all of the children on residence orders were formerly in long-term foster care, which is not the case for all children who are on residence orders. We should therefore be cautious about drawing conclusions from any comparisons between the children considered for special guardianship and those on residence orders.

With respect to these comparisons, the special guardianship group will only include those children already living with their carers at the time of data collection (n = 114), even if the special guardianship application had not yet been completed.

Characteristics and histories of the samples

Age

The children in the special guardianship sample were much younger, on average, than the children in our study of other permanent placements. This is undoubtedly due to differences in the way the samples were drawn. The ages of the children in the different permanent placement groups are shown in Table 8.1.

The mean age of the children considered for special guardianship was much lower than that of the children in other permanent placements, as shown in Table 8.2.

Given the younger age profile of the special guardianship sample and the stage in their lives at which they were studied, it is perhaps not surprising that, on average, they had been living with their current carers for a shorter period of time than those in other types of permanent placements, as shown in Table 8.3.

Despite these differences between the groups in relation to length of time in placement, we can nevertheless compare their ages when they

Table 8.1
Age at survey

Age in years	Carer adoption (n = 31) %	Stranger adoption (n = 43) %	Stable foster care (n = 63) %	Residence/special guardianship order (n = 15) %	Special guardianship (n = 114) %
0–2	–	–	–	–	18
3–6	–	–	–	–	33
7–9	16	56	6	19	20
10–12	45	25	26	38	15
13–15	19	14	52	38	12
16–18	16	5	16	6	2
24	3	–	–	–	–
Total	**100**	**100**	**100**	**100**	**100**

Table 8.2
Age in years of children in different permanent placements: mean (standard deviation)

Carer adoption (n = 31)	Stranger adoption (n = 43)	Stable foster care (n = 63)	Residence order (n = 15)	Special guardianship (n = 114)
12.4 (3.32)	10.1 (2.46)	13.4 (2.25)	12.06 (2.29)	6.9 (4.20)

entered those placements. The mean ages at which children moved to live with their current carers are shown in Table 8.4.

The mean age at which the children had moved to live with their prospective special guardians was 2.7 years, which was similar to the mean age at which the children in all other permanent placements had entered those placements. It approximated most closely to the age at which children in adoptive placements had entered their current placements. This suggests that, so far at least, special guardianship is not

189

Table 8.3
Time child has lived with current carers

Duration (years)	Carer adoption (n = 31) %	Stranger adoption (n = 43) %	Stable foster care (n = 63) %	Residence order (n = 15) %	Special guardianship (n = 114) %
<2	–	–	–		35
2–4	7	2	–		47
5–7	23	55	29	19	10
8 or more	70	43	71	81	8
Mean duration	8.74	7.26	8.84	3.81	3.1
(SD)	(2.65)	(1.31)	(1.97)	(.403)	(2.48)

Table 8.4
Age moved to live with current carers

	Mean age at entry to this placement Years (SD)
Adopted (all)	2.9 (3.1)
• adopted by stranger (n = 43)	2.6 (2.7)
• adopted by carer (n = 31)	3.6 (3.7)
Residence order (n = 16)	2.3 (2.1)
Stable foster care (n = 63)	4.1 (2.58)
Special guardianship (n = 106)	2.7 (1.31)

generally being used for older children and this may relate to its high use by kinship carers rather than unrelated foster carers.

Although the mean age at which children moved to their current carers was similar to the other groups, the range was very wide. The most common ages at which children had started living with their prospective special guardians was three to under seven years, accounting for 34 per cent of this sample. However, 26 per cent of these children had been living with their current carers since they were infants (under one year old) and two-fifths (40%) had moved to live with them before they were three years old. A substantial minority (26%) had moved to their current carers at a later stage, when they were between the ages of seven and 12.

Disability and health

Just under one-fifth of the children considered for special guardianship were reported by carers and/or social workers to have a physical or learning disability or sensory impairment. This was similar to the proportion of children with disabilities in our samples of children adopted by strangers or on residence orders, but lower than the proportions of those adopted by carers or in stable foster care, as shown in Table 8.5.

Table 8.5
Physical, sensory or learning impairments

	Carer adoption (n = 31) %	Stranger adoption (n = 43) %	Stable foster care (n = 63) %	Residence order (n = 15) %	Special guardianship (n = 114) %
Disabled	48 (15)	16 (7)	29 (18)	20 (3)	18 (20)

The most common type of disability was a learning disability, which was reported in relation to 13 per cent of the children in the special guardianship group, a figure identical to the percentage of those in the other types of permanent placements (13%).

The children in the special guardianship group appeared to be less likely to have chronic physical health problems than those in other permanent placements. These were reported in relation to just four per cent of the special guardianship group, compared to 14 per cent of those in other permanent placements.

Emotional and behavioural difficulties

We asked the carers and social workers of all the children to indicate whether they displayed any emotional and behavioural difficulties and to rate these on a four-point scale, which was taken from the Integrated

Children's System. Relatively few of the children subject to special guardianship applications appeared to have serious emotional and behavioural difficulties, compared to those in other types of permanent placements, as shown in Table 8.6.

Table 8.6
Ratings of emotional and behavioural development

	Carer adoption (n = 26) %	Stranger adoption (n = 37) %	Stable foster care (n = 56) %	Residence order (n = 13) %	Special guardianship (n = 103) %
Serious problems	4	13	12	8	5
Moderate problems	19	19	25	23	13
Some problems	35	30	27	31	48
No problems	42	38	36	38	34
Total	**100**	**100**	**100**	**100**	**100**

Just under one-fifth (18%) of the special guardianship children were rated as having moderate to severe emotional and behavioural difficulties, somewhat fewer than for those adopted by carers (23%) and markedly fewer than for those adopted by strangers (32%) or in long-term foster care (37%). However, it is possible that these lower ratings may be partly due to the younger overall age profile of the special guardianship group. For many children, emotional and behavioural difficulties may not emerge, or be reported, until they reach adolescence (Meltzer *et al*, 2000).

Reasons for separation from birth parents
We asked the social workers and carers involved in special guardianship applications to indicate the reasons that the child had come to live at this placement.[66] Respondents were able to select all reasons that applied in a particular case. In relation to the children adopted, fostered or on

---

[66] The findings from social workers and carers were merged to maximise the available data. Where information was collected from both sources in a particular case, the view of the carers was given priority as they were likely to know the child better.

residence orders, we asked the social workers for the main reason the child had last entered care, a somewhat different question. Our questions on whether parents were unable to care for the child were comparable for the two samples. However, we asked social workers of the fostered and adopted children whether abuse or neglect had led to the child becoming looked after. Questions about the children considered for special guardianship asked less specific questions about the presence of "risks to the safety of the child" or of a "failure to thrive" as proxy measures for abuse or neglect. With these caveats in mind, some comparisons are nevertheless possible.

For over one-half of the children who were the subject of special guardianship applications, the child was no longer living with birth parents because they were unable to care for him/her due to their own

Table 8.7
Reasons for separation from birth parents[67]

	Carer adoption (n = 19) %	Stranger adoption (n = 22) %	Stable foster care (n = 39) %	Residence order (n = 9) %	Special guardianship (n = 114) %
Parent unable to provide care	26	55	39	44	54
Risk to child's safety/actual or potential abuse	16	23	26	22	29
Failure to thrive/neglect	47	23	33	33	18

[67] Percentages in Table 8.7 do not total 100 per cent as not all main reasons have been included, only those that were broadly comparable across all four groups. The special guardianship group were not asked to provide a single main reason, but were asked to tick all boxes that applied. The three types of reasons presented above were therefore often overlapping factors leading to placement. To control for this to some degree, data on "risk to safety" and "failure to thrive" were calculated controlling for parent unable to provide care to avoid duplication.

disabilities or health, mental health or substance misuse problems (or a combination of these). In this respect, the circumstances of these children were similar to those of children adopted by strangers, as shown in Table 8.7.

There had also been concerns about the safety of the children with their birth parents for a similar proportion of those subject to special guardianship applications and concern about a failure to thrive was also in line with stranger adoptions. Although these comparisons are by no means exact, they do point to a degree of similarity in the circumstances leading to the separation of children in the special guardianship group to those in other types of permanent placement.

Family connections

Relative carers

Not surprisingly, when compared to children in long-term foster care, children who were the subject of special guardianship applications were far more likely to be living with relative carers, as shown in Table 8.8.

Table 8.8
Carer's relationship to child (n=196)

Type of placement	Stable foster care (n = 63)	Residence order (n = 15)	Special Guardianship (n = 114)
Birth relatives, of which:	36	67	84
• Grandparent	19	47	49
• Other relative	17	20	35
(Former) foster carers – not related	64	33	14
With other non-relatives	–	–	2

Across all types of permanent placement, the most common relative carers were grandparents. For all groups, the majority of other relative carers were the children's aunts or uncles.

Contact with birth parents

Not surprisingly, a much higher percentage of children who were subject to special guardianship applications had direct contact with birth parents compared to those who were adopted. Very few of the adopted children had face-to-face contact with a birth parent, and all but one of those who did was in the group adopted by their former foster carers. For the special guardianship group, patterns of contact with both their mothers and fathers were similar to those for the children on residence orders, as shown in Table 8.9.

Table 8.9
Face-to-face contact with parents

Contact with	Adopted (all) (n = 63) %	Stable foster care (n = 57) %	Residence order (n = 12) %	Special guardianship (n = 95) %
Mother	11	74	67	88
Father	6	37	58	60

The children in the special guardianship group were slightly more likely to see their mothers, and were much more likely to see their fathers, than children in long-term foster care. The proportion of children who saw their mothers regularly (at least monthly) was very much higher for the special guardianship group (55%) than was the case for children in all other forms of permanence, as shown in Table 8.10.

Table 8.11 indicates that one-third of the children in the special guardianship group (32%) saw their birth fathers at least monthly. They appeared much more likely to see them this frequently than either those in stable foster care or those on residence orders.

Table 8.10
Face-to-face contact with birth mother

	Adopted (n = 63) %	Stable foster care (n = 55) %	Residence order %	Special guardianship %
At least weekly	0	18	17	21
Monthly	2	13	0	34
Less often	10	42	50	34
Never	87	27	33	12

Table 8.11
Frequency of contact with birth father

	Adopted (n = 62) %	Stable foster care (n = 55) %	Residence order (n = 12) %	Special guardianship (n = 86) %
At least weekly	0	3	8	12
Monthly	2	9	–	20
Less often	5	24	50	28
Never	93	64	42	40

However, frequency of contact with birth parents tends to decrease over time in most substitute placements. In Chapter 6, we also identified a similar downward trend in levels of contact with birth parents over time once a special guardianship order had been made. Overall, these higher contact levels may relate to the intention of special guardianship to maintain a link between children and their birth parents. However, given that these children had, on average, lived for a shorter period of time with their carers when compared to those in other forms of permanent placement, it may be that the passage of time will further erode contact levels in special guardianship placements. It is simply too early to tell.

Overall, then, the children subject to special guardianship applications were more likely to be in regular contact with birth relatives than those in other types of permanent placement. They were more likely to be living with relative carers and more likely to have direct contact with both of their birth parents. These are hardly surprising findings, given the profile of those who have so far taken up special guardianship (relative carers) and the intention of the legislation.

Conclusion

Although the comparisons we have made between these different samples of children are not without considerable difficulty, they do provide an initial insight into the characteristics of children entering special guardianship families. In some respects, they serve to echo the findings presented in previous chapters. The children entering special guardianship are quite young, broadly as young as children entering adoptive placements. Although our comparisons are inexact, the children entering special guardianship also appear to come from similarly troubled family backgrounds where they have been at risk or where parents have been unable to provide care of sufficient quality. They are much more likely than other children to be living with relatives and to be in relatively close contact with their birth parents and other family members. Family relationships, and the problems to which they can give rise, are therefore at the centre of special guardianship. Finally, while special guardianship children manifest fewer emotional and behavioural problems than children in other permanent placements, this may be in part a feature of their relatively young age at the time of data collection.

In overall terms, therefore, special guardianship children appear to bear considerable resemblance to those children who enter the looked after system and then move on to adoption or, to a lesser extent, to long-term stable foster care. Their needs – and the services that may be required to meet them – are therefore also likely to be broadly similar. The fact that most take-up of special guardianship so far has concerned younger children in the public law arena makes these findings not too surprising. Why it is that broadly similar children take these different pathways needs to be a matter for further investigation.

Summary

- This chapter has compared the characteristics and circumstances of children for whom a special guardianship application had been made with those of children in other types of permanent placement, including those adopted, in long-term foster care and on residence orders. However, differences in the ways the special guardianship sample and the other permanent placements sample were drawn make direct comparisons between the two samples difficult.

- The average age of the children when they moved to live with their prospective special guardians was similar to the age at which children had entered other permanent placements, especially those entering adoptive placements. The young age of special guardianship children on entry to placement is likely to reflect the predominance of take-up by kinship carers in the context of public law proceedings.

- The proportion of children with disabilities in the special guardianship group was similar to that for children adopted by strangers and for those living with carers on residence orders, but it was lower than was the case for those in long-term foster care or adopted by carers. They were also less likely to have serious emotional and behavioural difficulties, although it is possible that this may be related to the younger age profile of the special guardianship group.

- For over half of the special guardianship group, one of the main reasons for separation from birth parents was their parents' inability to care for them due to mental health or substance abuse problems, or because of the parents' disabilities. The proportion separated for this reason was similar to that for children adopted by strangers and points to the complex family backgrounds of children entering special guardianship.

- The children subject to special guardianship applications were more likely to be in regular contact with birth relatives than those in other types of permanent placement. They were more likely to be living with relative carers and to have direct contact with their birth mothers and fathers, compared to children in other types of permanent placement.

9 Conclusion

The Adoption and Children Act 2002 provided the legal framework for special guardianship. From early 2006, it has provided an additional permanence option for children who cannot live with their birth parents. Special guardianship was intended to meet the needs of particular groups of children for whom the legal finality of adoption was not considered feasible or desirable. These groups included some children in settled placements with unrelated or kinship foster carers, in circumstances where a legal severance from their birth parents was neither wanted nor desirable, and some other children settled with relative carers outside the care system. They also included some children from minority ethnic communities, where adoption was not feasible, and unaccompanied asylum-seeking children, for whom greater legal security might be appreciated whilst allowing for their continuing loyalties to their birth families.

A special guardianship order is a powerful legal order. It invests in carers a high degree of parental responsibility, restricts that available to birth parents, lasts until the child is 18, and cannot be challenged without leave of the court. It therefore probably carries more power than that awarded to local authorities through care orders (Eddon, 2007). Children formerly looked after cease to be so and, apart from a responsibility to make provision for post-order support and services, local authorities cease to have direct powers of intervention. Although the regulatory framework governing services is extensive, guardians have no explicit entitlement to receive specific services. However, all local authorities do have an established duty of care and a failure to meet identified needs can be challenged through judicial review.

While the order cannot be challenged without leave of the court, there are no restrictions on parents or other relatives applying for contact, prohibited-steps or specific-issues orders, unless their right to do so is restricted by the court. In these respects, therefore, those obtaining special guardianship have less protection against further litigation than do those who adopt (Masson *et al*, 2008a).

From a research perspective, we know very little about how special guardianship is working out in practice. This research, commissioned as part of a wider study of permanent placements, represents a first attempt to see how special guardianship has been implemented in eight local authority areas, to identify some of the key challenges that have arisen, to assess who is taking it up, to describe the experiences of carers and children as they travel along the special guardianship road, to consider what may need to happen to make special guardianship work successfully for families and to gauge its potential impact on other permanent placement options for children. This chapter draws together some of the main findings from the policy study, surveys and interviews and considers some of the messages that arise for policy and practice.

Implementation

There is a high degree of goodwill towards special guardianship amongst childcare and social work professionals. Most practitioners felt that it could provide children and their carers with sufficient parental responsibility, legal security and autonomy from local authority interference to guarantee a good degree of permanence for families that want this. Overwhelmingly, carers involved in the study also welcomed it. Despite the challenges that lay ahead and continuing concerns about financial security and the services that were available, most reported that, in hindsight, the order was broadly meeting their expectations and that it had been the right decision for them and their children.

Recent research has alerted us to variations in the way that local authorities and the social work teams that work within them vary in their use of different placement resources (Sinclair *et al*, 2007). It would therefore be surprising if the use of special guardianship was an exception. The speed with which these local authorities had risen to the challenges of special guardianship was highly variable.[68] Some had given themselves a good head start, by preparing policies and procedures and

---

[68] This was reflected in the number of referrals made to the study by different local authorities, ranging from four to 60 within the research timeframe.

earmarking resources at an early stage. Others had appeared more reluctant to invest. One key factor that helped to accelerate change was the presence (or otherwise) of a strong sense of corporate leadership and the presence of senior lead officers to champion special guardianship across the authority. Where this leadership was lacking, progress had been slower and was less likely to have become embedded in local practice. Area demographics, the pressures created by other priorities and initiatives, and the time needed to scope demand and resources and make shifts in prevailing staff cultures and assumptions also played their part in delaying or accelerating change.

The differences between local authorities were also evident in the structure and organisation of teams. Each local authority had different arrangements for responding to special guardianship applications. Only in one area did a single team handle all cases referred to the authority through to the final court hearing. In all other areas, the teams that were involved depended on the type of case – whether it concerned a looked after child, whether the child was in kinship or unrelated foster care, whether it was a child "in need" or whether it was a "private" application from kinship carers not previously known to the local authority. There was also a similar diversity in relation to the provision of post-order support services. In general, where a dedicated social work team was involved at all stages before and after the hearing, the pathways for carers appeared clearer, pools of expertise could be developed, and services tended to be more coherent and comprehensive. In areas where a range of generic teams was involved, pathways and services appeared more fragmented. As with adoption and kinship care, therefore, there is a good case for specialisation.

Take-up – who is applying and why?

Some commentators anticipated that special guardianship would appeal to family and friends carers. To date, this has proven to be the case. The policy study revealed that most take-up in the first two years had been from relatives, with grandparents in the majority. The children concerned were younger than might have been anticipated, most came from troubled family backgrounds, and the majority of cases had arisen in the public law arena.[69] These perceptions were confirmed by the survey findings. Over four-fifths of applications concerned relatives (86%), over one-half involved grandparents (53%), and one-half (52%) involved children aged five years or younger. Most of the children (74%) were already living with the carer prior to application, the majority (65%) for two years or more. Over two-thirds (70%) had been looked after immediately before application, just under one-half (48%) in kinship foster care, and the remainder in unrelated foster care. Most children came from troubled family backgrounds. For the majority (68%), there had been concerns about maltreatment (often leading to care entry) and significant minorities of birth parents were struggling with alcohol or drug dependency, mental health problems and, perhaps to a lesser degree, with domestic violence.

Special guardianship is therefore being used with a broader range of younger children than perhaps was originally envisaged. Most cases have occurred in the public law arena as either an exit strategy from care or as an alternative to care and, subsequently, adoption for the youngest children. Although the primary motivations for carers seeking special guardianship were to provide the child with a permanent stable home and to have greater control over decisions affecting them and greater legal security, a desire to keep the child within the family network or return them to it figured with equal prominence.

All things being equal, keeping children within the family network is a good thing. Recent developments in law and policy are encouraging local authorities to explore the potential for placement within the extended family network before initiating care proceedings or entry to care, whenever it is safe to do so.[70] However, the profile of relative carers

---

[69] Many practitioners who participated in policy interviews had anticipated that special guardianship would be used primarily with older settled children no longer in need of services. This has not so far proved to be the case.

[70] See the *Public Law Outline 2008* (Ministry of Justice, 2008) and the recently revised *Children Act 1998, Guidance and Regulations, Volume 1* (*Court Orders*) (Department for Children, Schools and Families, 2008a). However, the tragic death of "Baby Peter" has also made councils more risk averse and led to some increase in care proceedings (see *Community Care*, 27 November 2008, p. 5).

and children seeking special guardianship does raise important questions about the durability of placements as carers and children age, the reduced opportunities for children to find adoptive placements should breakdowns occur at a later point, and the resource implications involved in providing longer-term services to meet enduring needs. Some service providers had recognised the importance of providing an appropriate service structure to enable special guardianship families to provide long-term care more successfully. Others, however, had been taken aback by the level of service demand and questioned the appropriateness of special guardianship in more complex cases where ongoing support was needed.

In contrast, take-up by unrelated foster carers caring for older children has been low, accounting for only 13 per cent of our survey sample. Factors that have inhibited take-up include concerns about financial security, loss of structured social work support for them and the child (now and in the future), and responsibility for managing birth family relationships (see also Hall, 2008; Schofield, 2008). Some unrelated and kinship foster carers also have concerns about the support that might be available to their children as they transition to adulthood. Leaving care entitlements for looked after children have been greatly strengthened in recent years and, while previously looked after special guardianship children may be entitled to some support as "qualifying" children, there is a need for greater clarity about what this will mean for them in practice.

In an effort to encourage take-up, some areas were starting to offer foster carers guaranteed financial and support packages for the duration of placements. The costs of doing so for local authorities were high, though certainly not higher than keeping the child in the looked after system. There was limited evidence that unaccompanied asylum-seeking children were being considered, but there was some encouragement with regard to minority ethnic communities in areas with sizeable minority ethnic populations.

Pathways to special guardianship – assessment and the courts

The appropriateness of a family placement will depend to a large degree on the quality of assessment that is undertaken and the degree to which sufficient safeguards exist to quality assure the decisions being made. In these respects, the findings were mixed. Carers gave high priority to the provision of reliable advice, information and guidance to help them steer a steady course through proceedings. This was frequently in short supply, in part due to the relative newness of the order and the limited awareness of the social workers upon whom they primarily relied, especially in areas where practice guidance and professional training were not readily available. Where accurate advice was lacking, heavy reliance was placed on solicitors and children's guardians as alternative sources of information and support.

Many children had been settled with their foster carers (unrelated or kinship) for some time at the point of application. In these circumstances, the decision to seek special guardianship was usually the result of discussions at planning meetings and reviews. The assessment process and court report could then build on the assessments that had already been undertaken under fostering regulations, although some foster carers still experienced the process as intrusive and repetitive.

Where children had not been looked after and, in particular, where assessments had not previously been undertaken, the policy study revealed considerable concern amongst practitioners about the short time-scales for completing assessments and court reports (commonly 12 weeks or fewer).[71] Although this could bring a sharp focus to the work, it often left insufficient time for in-depth coverage, reflection and analysis. In some instances, social workers felt that they had to play catch-up after the event – re-visiting assessment areas after the order had been granted. In these respects, special guardianship assessments tended to be contrasted unfavourably to those required for adoption and fostering, where more time was available to assess suitability and to prepare carers adequately for the task ahead.

For some children the timescales could also build certain risks into the system. Where children were moving from foster care to relatives with

---

[71] Over two-thirds of children in this sample (70%) were looked after at time of application, just over half in unrelated foster care. Thirty per cent were living with relatives on residence orders (19) or informally with no order (17).

whom they had not previously lived or where they were already living with relatives without legal protection, there were concerns about existing safeguards. Some practitioners queried whether it would be helpful if there was provision for trial placements and for pre-assessment plans for the child, consistent with those in adoption, to ensure that these permanence decisions were safe and right for the child.[72]

Safeguards are also written in through quality assurance procedures. In two areas, special guardianship recommendations in public law cases were subject to the scrutiny of permanence panels before going to court. In others, decisions were signed off by a senior officer. However, it was not always clear how "private" applications concerning children not previously known to children's services were quality assured, if at all. Given the powerful nature of the order and the limited rights of local authorities to intervene once the order is made, there is a case for further guidance to clarify and strengthen safeguarding arrangements in special guardianship cases. Safeguarding concerns were uppermost in the minds of social workers, reinforced by recent child tragedies, and most were trying to exercise control and scrutiny in circumstances where it was difficult to achieve it satisfactorily.

The survey findings were, however, rather more encouraging. Most carers felt that the core areas of assessment had been covered in sufficient depth, although rather more weight had been given to their suitability rather than the child's needs. Indeed, some carers were frustrated by delays in the process, its overly intrusive nature, and the duplication of information where they had already been long-standing foster carers or the child had been living with them for some time. These are difficult questions. Many relative carers have not chosen to care or, in the case of grandparents, to resume a caring role. They are frequently thrust into the role through family circumstances. Many do not want to be mainstream foster carers (or would not pass the more stringent assessments required), nor do they necessarily want to have an enduring link with the local authority, beyond the particular support they may need (see also Hunt,

---

[72] These suggestions from practitioners would, however, require legislative reform as they would conflict with special guardianship as a private law order.

2003; Broad, 2007; Farmer and Moyers, 2008). Getting this balance right is a major challenge facing local authorities when approving family carers. On the one hand, there is a clear need for a robust and comprehensive assessment process to safeguard children, especially with respect to the parenting capacity of carers. On the other, assessment also needs to have a flexible and inclusive format that is not off-putting to family carers. In this respect, the assessment tools that are being piloted for use in kinship settings may prove helpful.[73]

Once the court decision had been made, the response of carers was overwhelmingly positive. Only one carer continued to feel that adoption would have been a preferred alternative, and there were some who had felt pressure to accept special guardianship. Other court orders quite commonly accompanied the making of the special guardianship order. In just over one-quarter of cases (26%), a contact order was made or changed and in one in nine cases (11%), a supervision order had been attached. Supervision orders tended to be used to ensure access to local authority resources and support during the early stages of placement, especially where relationships with birth family members were conflicted, or where particular concerns were identified by the court. Whether orders of this kind should be necessary in special guardianship cases is a matter for discussion, although it probably relates to the abruptness with which some orders are made or the caution exercised by the courts in some cases.

Experiences

At the point of data collection, most carers (76%) and social workers (83%) reported that the placements had gone "very well". There were few social work concerns about the safety of children and social workers reported a high degree of commitment to the placement by carers (96%) and children (89%). Birth parents appeared more ambivalent, with only

---

[73] The assessment tool is being developed by Family Rights Group in partnership with BAAF and the Fostering Network: http://www.frg.org.uk/family_and_friends_care_assessment.html.

44 per cent reported as being "fully" committed. Most children were reported to be faring well, especially in relation to their health, attachments and emotional well-being. However, overall well-being was lower for older children and, in some respects, for children with learning disabilities and those living in unrelated foster care settings. While some children (mostly younger) were described by carers as relatively easy to care for, concerns about attachment, emotional and behavioural difficulties were quite common. Children of school age also appeared to be faring less well in education than in some other developmental areas.

From the carers' perspective, special guardianship was broadly meeting their expectations. They felt that it provided them with sufficient parental control and legal security while enabling the children to retain a link with birth parents. Where children had been living with their carers for some time, the transition to special guardianship had not always greatly disturbed the pattern of everyday relationships. Some unrelated and kinship foster carers and their children welcomed the normalisation of family relationships, as they were, to a degree, liberated from the inevitable constraints imposed upon children and their carers by the care system.

The resumption of a caring role, however, had a considerable material and psychological impact on some kinship carers and their families (see also Broad, 2007; Hunt et al, 2008). The life plans of carers, especially grandparents, had to be adjusted. Some had given up employment and most sacrificed significant aspects of their social lives. Some kinship carers also struggled with ambivalent feelings towards their own children, perhaps especially where maltreatment was evident. Although for some kinship carers, contact with birth parents was relatively unproblematic, for others, the management of birth family relationships was a significant and stressful challenge. While kinship carers relied heavily (and often preferred to rely) on informal support from family and friends, fault-lines sometimes occurred within families, thereby reducing the potential for practical support or help with childcare and respite.

Support and services

Given these experiences, many special guardians and their children will need some continuing professional support. As we have seen, however, not all special guardianship applicants have an entitlement to receive an assessment of their support needs and local authorities are not obliged to provide specific services when needs are identified (Jordan and Lindley, 2006; Masson *et al*, 2008a). It was therefore encouraging to find that most carers (80%) had received some form of needs assessment, although depth of coverage was variable. Most had been undertaken in advance of the court hearing. This is important. It is difficult to see how carers can make a rational judgement about the appropriateness of special guardianship to their circumstances if they are not made fully aware in advance of the services (financial and practical) that will be provided. Having said this, there were instances where needs identified and agreed in the support plan did not translate into discrete services once the order was made.

The policy study revealed how local authority differences in implementation, structure and organisation had made a deep imprint on the services that were provided, to whom they applied and for how long. Practitioners in areas where take-up of special guardianship had been higher also emphasised the relatively high level of demand for services and the consequent resource strains placed on specialist post-order support teams. In one or two areas, consideration was being given to a realignment of resources from post-adoption to special guardianship support as the balance in the workload was gradually changing. Should special guardianship applications continue on their upward curve, this re-balancing would become a live issue for many more local authorities, unless fresh resources are released to fund special guardianship support specifically.

At the point of data collection, most social workers were no longer in touch with special guardianship families (61%). This decline in support is consistent with research on kinship care more generally. For some carers, case closure had occurred abruptly once the order was made, even where assurances had been made to the contrary. For others, loss of contact had not been unwelcome. Not all carers wanted or expected continuing support and the value of self-reliance was consistently highlighted in interviews. Where contact did continue, it was often highly valued and tended to be more intensive in the first few months after the order had been granted to enable children and families to settle, supervise family contact (where this was necessary or required by the court), and arrange access to other services. As we have seen, supervision orders were sometimes used to ensure access to these resources.

In relation to specific services, the survey findings pointed to some priority areas. Beyond access to accurate advice, information and financial support, it highlighted the value of support and mediation to help carers manage often quite complex and conflicted birth family relationships, therapeutic input to help understand and manage the challenging behaviour of children, and support groups, training and social activities for them and their children. Very little use was made of respite care (6%). Most carers preferred to rely on family and friends, although in one-fifth of cases (21%) it had never been offered. Some who had been promised respite reported that it had never materialised, although their need for it remained great. One-third of children (34%) had received some therapeutic input, mainly from CAMHS, and well over half (61%) of carers had received support in relation to birth family contact. The frequency and complex nature of this contact was identified by practitioners as the most resource-intensive and difficult dimension of post-order services. Training needs for carers had been particularly ill considered during assessment and while 32 per cent of carers had attended a support group, these were rarely focused specifically on special guardians.

Specialist teams tended to have a range of informal strategies for staying in touch, even where allocated workers were no longer active. Informal support groups, newsletters and social events provided easier routes back into services for carers experiencing difficulties at a later point. Informality and flexibility are important. Kinship carers can be reluctant to ask for help, sometimes out of concern that they will be perceived as not coping (Bullard et al, 1991; Hunt et al, 2008), and simply providing a signpost to a duty service, as often happened, presents barriers to access that some find difficult to overcome.

Concerns about the financial implications of caring for children have deterred unrelated foster carers from taking up special guardianship and are a major worry for kinship carers, who have often received lower allowances (Waterhouse and Brocklesby, 1999; Broad, 2007; Hall, 2008; Schofield *et al*, 2008). The policy study revealed the variability that existed in financial arrangements across the eight local authorities – and within them with respect to different types of applicants. In general, entitlements for former foster carers (unrelated and kinship) tended to be greater. For these carers, allowances were more likely to be protected for at least two years and, in some cases, for the duration of placement. Entitlements, if they existed at all, were much more varied for carers of children who had not previously been looked after or were not previously known to children's services. The benchmarking of payments was also not consistent. In some areas, allowances were linked to the fostering rate (as advised in official guidance and case law).[74] In others, it was linked to lower rates paid to adopters or those holding residence orders. Inconsistency was therefore the norm.

The survey findings offered some encouragement. Most special guardians (90%) were in receipt of a regular allowance, one-half (50%) had received assistance with legal fees and smaller proportions had received other forms of financial assistance, including settling-in grants or assistance with childcare costs or costs associated with birth family contact. There was little evidence of carers receiving large lump sums or pressuring local authorities for additional resources (see also Hunt *et al*, 2008). Many former foster carers were still financially worse off, since they were generally subject to an annual means test and important fringe benefits, such as holiday and birthday money or school clothes allowances were no longer routinely paid. Obtaining assistance was often fraught. There was evidence in some areas of attempts by local authorities to negotiate allowances downwards and sometimes satisfactory solutions were found only after the protracted intervention of solicitors or the courts.

Resourcing special guardianship services is a challenge for local authorities. Where it is being used for older children in settled long-term foster placements or where the alternative would be to bring a child into

---

[74] See: Department for Education and Skills, 2005. The relevant appeal court judgment is: *B v London Borough of Lewisham* [2008] EWHC 738 (Admin).

the system, the cost implications of financial and support packages are likely to be relatively neutral or, perhaps, more favourable to the local authority. Where this is not the case, the implications for local authorities are serious. Their reluctance to enter into long-term financial agreements with some relative carers, whose expectations may be raised by advice from solicitors or the courts, is perhaps understandable when the level of future demand is unknown. Many practitioners identified a need for further guidance to help clarify local authority responsibilities in this area and some questioned where the boundaries lay between local and central state responsibilities for providing income maintenance to families caring for the children of others (see also Hunt *et al*, 2008).

Comparing special guardianship children to those in other permanent placements

Initial comparisons between the characteristics and circumstances of special guardianship children and children long-term fostered or adopted by carers or strangers reveal both similarities and differences. Of course, differences in the way the samples were drawn make these comparisons at best tentative; like was not being compared with like. One inevitable feature of this sampling was that special guardianship children were younger and had been living with their carers on average for a shorter length of time.

However, the mean age at which these children moved to live with their current and prospective special guardians (2.7 years) was very similar to that for children adopted (2.9 years) but younger than for those who went into long-term foster care (4.1 years). The relatively young age of children entering special guardianship has been highlighted throughout this report.

Children in special guardianship households were rather less likely to have physical, learning or sensory impairments, although the proportion (18%) was very close to that for children adopted by strangers (16%). They also appeared less likely to have moderate to severe emotional or behavioural difficulties than children in all other groups. However, these differences may in part be explained by their younger age at the point of data collection.

Comparisons in relation to reasons for placement were rather more difficult to make, since the questions asked did not correspond exactly. Having said this, the background circumstances of children across all permanent placements bore signs of similarity with respect to maltreatment and to the problems experienced by birth parents, including physical and mental ill health and, often in combination with these, problems with alcohol and/or drug dependency.

In overall terms, therefore, children entering the range of permanent placements appear to have a good amount in common with respect to their past family experiences, the legacies these are likely to have for children and their carers and the challenges that carers are likely to face. Indeed, these quite often appear to be broadly the same children taking different pathways. It would therefore be reasonable to view special guardianship as properly part of the continuum of permanent placements available to children and families. It is equally reasonable to assume, given the profile of carers and children, that these placements should be adequately supported and in a similar way to those of children taking alternative pathways. Herein lies the rub. Historically, the resources of local authorities have tended to be focused more heavily on the relatively small group of children who are within the care system. Proportionately far fewer resources have been provided to those who are diverted from it or to those who exit it through family reunification, adoption or residence. The risk will be that special guardianship will follow this route. While it undoubtedly offers a valuable permanence option for some (perhaps many) children, like adoption, it is much more likely to work successfully if it is adequately resourced and carers are sufficiently supported to deliver the care that children need.

Anticipating the future

It is still too early to predict where special guardianship will go in the future. However, it is very likely that the regulatory framework surrounding services will be influential. This is what is attracting relative carers to seek special guardianship over residence orders. It is also part of what has held back long-term foster carers from considering it more seriously and in greater numbers. Most policy interviewees felt that residence was an unattractive option in comparison. The number of residence orders granted has declined in recent years, and most predicted that it would decline further. It is here that special guardianship may have its most obvious impact.

More children may also be diverted from the care system. Kinship carers often viewed the need to keep children within the family and prevent them leaving the network through long-term care or stranger adoption as an important motivating factor in seeking or accepting special guardianship. If the upward curve in applications continues, it is likely that more children will be placed with relatives in this way. As we have seen, this is also in line with recent government initiatives that encourage local authorities to explore the potential within family networks before care proceedings are initiated. If this does prove to be the case, then strategies to ensure the safety and success of these placements are likely to become an even bigger policy priority.

More children may also leave the system through special guardianship. As we have seen, the majority of children in this study were looked after immediately before the application was made. Special guardianship was therefore being used as an exit strategy. Should it continue to be used for very young children, it is also likely that there will be some impact on adoptions. Policy interviewees had mixed views in this regard. Some had noticed an impact on adoption by family members, others had not yet seen one, but this impact was not because the courts were necessarily set against it. Indeed, the relevant appeal court judgments have clarified that each case should turn on its own merits (Bedingfield, 2007; Bond, 2007). However, a decision for special guardianship may be more likely where birth parents are in agreement and do not present a risk to the stability of the placement:

> *It's the risk that the parents pose to the child . . . If the parents accept the placement and are not going to try to disrupt it, either by physical acts or by making repeated court applications, then special guardianship should be fine. But if they are going to try and disrupt the placement, then [the court] would be looking at adoption to get anonymity for the child and get the safeguards that you have with adoption.*
> (Childcare solicitor)

Where local authorities invest time in seeking out willing family members at an early stage, this may also have some impact on adoption. As we have seen, when faced with a choice between adoption and special guardianship, some family members chose the latter because it was less disruptive to the structure of family relationships. A few had experienced a degree of coercion. Some birth parents objected to adoption but were prepared to agree to special guardianship, perhaps because they hoped it would be less permanent. In these circumstances, special guardianship sometimes offered a quicker and easier solution. It is likely that all these factors will be at play in the future to some degree.

Although there has been some fall in adoption rates in recent years, it is not at all clear why this has been the case. What is quite likely is that special guardianship will eat into these figures in the future. In many cases, this will be perfectly appropriate. In others, it may raise concerns. The long-term security of special guardianship placements has not yet been tested. A number of policy interviewees worried about this permanence question. We know that placement breakdowns are more likely to occur in adolescence. If this pattern does emerge, many children might well have lost a chance for permanence elsewhere. The best protection against this is to ensure that assessments are robust and carers well prepared and that there is an adequate service structure in place to meet both existing needs and those that may arise as the placement progresses. Although carers valued their independence, most also wanted a port of call when the seas turned choppy.

It is also clear that the long-term security of special guardianship as a permanence option for children needs to be tested through research. This is amongst the first studies on special guardianship and its limitations have been made clear. It has covered only the first two years of this new provision. It has inevitably been exploratory in design and descriptive-analytic in approach. It has examined many issues arising from the bedding-in process and, perhaps more importantly, traced the characteristics and experiences of the first cohort of carers and children as they travelled along this pathway. At this relatively early stage, the signs were quite encouraging.

The study has not been able to say whether these were the *right* placement decisions for these children. That can only be assessed over a longer period of time using a more rigorous outcomes design, perhaps also comparing the durability and quality of special guardianship placements to those found in other forms of permanent placement. Studies of this kind would give us a much clearer picture about which children in what circumstances might benefit most from special guardianship (as opposed to other options) and about the longer-term needs that arise from the profile (especially the age profile) of children and guardians and from the nature and management of children's long-term relationships with their birth families. Such a programme of research would help us to understand more adequately the particular place of special guardianship within the continuum of permanence options for children and to assess more clearly its relative impact on other forms of permanence.

References

Adcock M. and White R. (1985) 'Adoption, custodianship or fostering?', *Adoption & Fostering*, 9:4, pp 114–118

Altshuler, S. (1999) 'The well-being of children in kinship foster care', in Gleeson J. and Hairston C. (eds), *Kinship Care: Improving practice through research*, Washington DC: CWLA Press

Bainham A. (2007) 'Permanence for children: special guardianship or adoption?', The Cambridge Law Journal, 66, pp 520–523

Bedingfield D. (2007) 'Adoption or special guardianship? The impact of Re S, Re AJ and Re M-J', *Family Law Week*, February, accessed at: www.familylaw week.co.uk/site.aspx?i=ed563

Beek M. and Schofield G (2004) *Providing a Secure Base in Long-Term Foster Care*, London: BAAF

Berridge D. (1997) *Foster Care: A research review*, London: The Stationery Office

Berridge D., Beecham J., Brodie I., Cole T., Daniels H., Knapp M. and Macneill V. (2002) 'Costs and consequences of services for trouble adolescents: an exploratory, analytic study', Luton: University of Luton

Biehal N. (2005) *Working with Adolescents: Supporting families, preventing breakdown*, London: BAAF

Biehal N., Clayden J., Stein M. and Wade J (1995) *Moving On: Young people and leaving care schemes*, London: HMSO

Biehal N., Ellison S., Sinclair I. and Baker C. (2010) *Belonging and Permanence: Outcomes in Long-Term Foster Care and Adoption*, London: BAAF

Bond A (2007) 'Special guardianship after Re S, Re AJ and Re M-J', *Family Law*, pp 321–325

Broad B. (2001) 'Kinship care: supporting children in placements with extended family and friends', *Adoption & Fostering*, 25, pp 33–41

Broad B. (2007) 'Kinship care: what works? Who cares?', *Social Work and Social Sciences Review*, 13:1, pp 59–74

Broad B., Hayes R. and Rushworth C. (2001) *Kith and Kin: Kinship care for vulnerable young people*, York: Joseph Rowntree Foundation/National Children's Bureau

Bullard E. (1991) 'Custodianship and its implications for the Children Act', *Children and Society*, 5:2, pp 136–145

Bullard E., Malos E. and Parker R. (1991) *Custodianship: Caring for other people's children*, London: HMSO

Cabinet Office (2000) *The Prime Minister's Review: Adoption: Issues for consultation*, London: Cabinet Office

Clarke L. and Cains H. (2001) 'Grandparents and the care of children: the research evidence', in Broad B. (ed.) *Kinship Care: The placement*, Lyme Regis: Russell House Publishing

Department for Children, Schools and Families (2008a) *Children Act 1989, Guidance and Regulations, Volume 1 (Court Orders)*, London: DCSF

Department for Children, Schools and Families (2008b) *Statistical First Release: Children looked after in England (including adoption and care leavers) year ending 31st March 2008*, London: DCSF

Department for Education and Skills (2005) *Special Guardianship Guidance: Children Act 1989: The special guardianship regulations 2005*, London: DfES

Department for Education and Skills (2006) *Care Matters: Transforming the lives of children and young people in care*, London: DfES

Department for Education and Skills (2007) *Care Matters: Time for change*, London: DfES

Department for Education and Skills (2008) *Statistical First Release, Special educational needs in England*, London: DCSF

Department of Health (2000a) *Adoption: A new approach*, London: Department of Health

Department of Health (2000b) *Framework for the Assessment of Children in Need and their Families*, London: The Stationery Office

Department of Health (2001) *Children (Leaving Care) Act 2000: Regulations and Guidance*, London: DH

Eddon G. (2006) 'Placing children with family members', *Family Law*, November, pp 948–952

Eddon G. (2007) 'Special guardianship: imaginative use?', *Family Law*, pp 169–170

Farmer E. and Moyers S. (2008) *Kinship Care: Fostering effective family and friends placements*, London: Jessica Kingsley Publishers

Finch J. (1989) *Family Obligations and Social Change*, Cambridge, Polity Press

Fratter J., Rowe J., Sapsford D. and Thoburn J. (1991) *Permanent Family Placement: A decade of experience*, London: BAAF

Gibbs I., Sinclair I. and Stein M. (2005) 'Children and young people in and leaving care', in Bradshaw J. and Mayhew E. (eds), *The Wellbeing of Children in the UK*, London: Save the Children

Gleeson J., O'Donnell J. and Bonecuter F. (1997) 'Understanding the complexity of practice in kinship foster care', *Child Welfare*, 76:6, pp 801–826

Gray A. (2005) 'The changing availability of grandparents as carers and its implications for childcare policy in the UK', *Journal of Social Policy*, 34:4, pp 557–577

Greeff R. (ed) (1999) *Fostering Kinship: An international perspective on kinship foster care*, Brookfield, CT: Ashgate

Hall A. (2008) 'Special guardianship and permanency planning: unforeseen consequences and missed opportunities', *Child and Family Law Quarterly*, 20:3, pp 359–377

Harwin J., Owen M., Locke R. and Forrester D. (2003) *Making Care Orders Work: A study of care plans and their implementation*, London: The Stationery Office

Hunt J. (2003) *Family and Friends Carers: Scoping paper prepared for the Department of Health*, London: DH

Hunt J., Waterhouse S. and Lutman E. (2008) *Keeping them in the Family: Outcomes for children placed in kinship care through care proceedings*, London: BAAF

Jackson S. (2002) 'Promoting stability and continuity in care away from home', in McNeish D., Newman T. and Roberts R. (eds), *What Works for Children?*, Buckingham: Open University Press

Jordan L. and Lindley B. (2006) 'Special guardianship: an overview of the legal framework', in Jordan L. and Lindley B. (eds), *Special Guardianship: What does it offer children who cannot live with their parents?*, London: Family Rights Group

Kelly S., Whiteley D., Sipe T. and Yorker B. (2000) 'Psychological distress in grandmother kinship care providers: the role of resources, social support and physical health', *Child Abuse and Neglect*, 24, pp 311–321

Laws S. (2001) 'Looking after children within the extended family: carers' views', in Broad B. (ed.) *Kinship Care: The placement choice for children and young people*, Lyme Regis: Russell House Publishing

Lowe N., Murch M., Bader K., Borkowski M., Copner R., Lisles C. and Shearman J. (2002) *The Plan for the Child: Adoption or long-term fostering*, London: BAAF

Masson J., Bailey-Harris R. and Probert R. (2008a) *Cretney's Principles of Family Law*, London: Sweet and Maxwell

Masson J., Pearce J. and Bader K. (2008b) *Care Profiling Study, Ministry of Justice Research Series 4/08*, London: Ministry of Justice

Meltzer H., Gatward R., Goodman R. and Ford T. (2000) *The Mental Health of Children and Adolescents in Great Britain*, London: The Stationery Office

Millham S., Bullock R., Hosie K. and Little M. (1986) *Lost in Care: The problem of maintaining links between children in care and their families*, Gower: Aldershot

Ministry of Justice (2008) *The Public Law Outline: Guide to case management in public law proceedings*, London: Ministry of Justice

Newman T. and Blackburn S. (2002) *Transitions in the Lives of Children and Young People: Resilience factors. Interchange 78*, Edinburgh: Scottish Executive Education Department

Packman J. and Hall C. (1998) *From Care to Accommodation*, London: The Stationery Office

Parkinson P. (2003) 'Child protection, permanency planning and children's right to family life', *International Journal of Law, Policy and Family*, 17:2, pp 147–172

Quinton D., Rushton A., Dance C. and Mayes D. (1997) 'Contact between children placed away from home and their birth parents: research issues and evidence', *Clinical Child Psychology and Psychiatry*, 2, pp 393–1045

Rushton A. (2003) 'Local authority and voluntary adoption agencies' arrangements for supporting adoptive families: a survey of practice', *Adoption & Fostering*, 27:3, pp 51–60

Schofield G., Beek M. Sargent K. and Thoburn J. (2000) *Growing up in Foster Care*, London: BAAF

Schofield G., Thoburn J., Howell D. and Dickens J. (2007) 'The search for stability and permanence: modelling the pathways of long-stay looked after children', *British Journal of Social Work*, 37:4, p 14

Schofield G., Ward E., Warman A., Simmonds J. and Butler J. (2008) *Permanence in Foster Care: A study of care planning and practice in England and Wales*, London: BAAF

Selwyn J., Sturgess W., Quinton D. and Baxter C. (2006) *Costs and Outcomes of Non-Infant Adoptions*, London: BAAF

Selwyn J. and Wijedasa D. (2009) 'The placement of looked after minority ethnic children', in Schofield G. and Simmonds J. (eds), *The Child Placement Handbook: Research, policy and practice*, London: BAAF

Shaw C. (1998) *Remember my Messages*, London: Who Cares? Trust

Sinclair I. (2005) *Fostering Now: Messages from research*, London: Jessica Kingsley Publishers

Sinclair I., Baker C., Lee J. and Gibbs I. (2007) *The Pursuit of Permanence: A study of the English care system*, London: Jessica Kingsley Publishers

Sinclair I., Baker C., Wilson K. and Gibbs I. (2005c) *Foster Children. Where they go and how they get on*, London: Jessica Kingsley Publishers

Sinclair I., Gibbs I. and Wilson K. (2005a) *Foster carers: Why they stay and why they leave*, London: Jessica Kingsley Publishers

Sinclair I., Wilson K. and Gibbs I. (2005b) *Foster Placements: Why they succeed and why they fail*, London: Jessica Kingsley Publishers

Social Exclusion Unit (2003) *A Better Education for Children in Care*, London: Office of the Deputy Prime Minister

Thoburn J. (2002) *Adoption and Permanence for Children who Cannot Live Safely with Birth Parents or Relatives*, London: Department of Health, Making Research Count, Research in Practice

Triseliotis J. (2002) 'Long-term fostering or adoption? The evidence examined', *Child and Family Social Work*, 7:1, pp 23–34

Wade J. (2006) 'Support for young people leaving care in the UK', in McAuley C., Pecora P. and Rose W. (eds), *Enhancing the Wellbeing of Children and Families through Effective Interventions – UK and USA evidence for practice*, London: Jessica Kingsley Publishers

Wade J. (2008) 'The ties that bind: support from birth families and substitute families for young people leaving care', *British Journal of Social Work*, 38:1, pp 39–54

Wade J., Mitchell F. and Baylis G. (2005) *Unaccompanied Asylum Seeking Children: The response of social work services*, London: BAAF

Ward H. and Skuse T. (2001) 'Performance targets and stability of placements for children long looked after away from home', *Children and Slociety*, 15, pp 333–346

Ward P. (2004) 'Achieving permanence for looked after children through special guardianship: a study of the experience of New Zealand guardians with implications for special guardianship in England', *Adoption & Fostering*, 28:4, pp 16–26

Waterhouse S. and Brocklesby E. (1999) 'Placement choices for children: giving more priority to kinship placements', in Greeff R. (ed.) *Fostering Kinship: An international perspective on kinship foster care*, Aldershot: Ashgate

Wheelock J. and Jones K. (2002) 'Grandparents are the next best thing: informal childcare for working parents in urban Britin', *Journal of Social Policy*, 31:3, pp 441–463

Index

Compiled by Elisabeth Pickard

Please note: SG stands for special guardianship, throughout the index